SURVIVAL ENGLISH

International Communication for Professional People

PETER VINEY
JOHN CURTIN

Heinemann

Contents Chart

Business

Socializing

Travel

Hotels

Money

Food & Drink

TOPIC	UNIT	COMMUNICATIVE AIMS	GRAMMAR PRACTICE *	VOCABULARY
	1 Taxi!	Taking a cab. Personal conversation. Paying and tipping.	*Be:* present & past. Prepositions. *Which?*	Currency.
	2 Mr. Robertson Arrives	Identifying yourself. Introductions and greetings. 'Breaking the ice'.	*How? I'll.*	Greetings.
	3 Appointments and Dates	Arriving for appointments. Talking about dates.	*Have.* Present continuous (for future). Present simple (for future).	Places. Dates. Times. Ordinal numbers.
	4 Arrangements	Telephoning. Making appointments.	*I'd like to. Can? Could? Going to.*	Places. Days. Times.
	5 What do you do?	Describing jobs. Asking and answering questions about people. Answering questions about yourself.	Present simple. *She was born.* Questions.	Jobs. Titles. Nationality.
	6 Office Supplies	Making out orders. Letter-writing. Expressing quantity.	*There is/are some.* (Un)Countable nouns.	Numbers. Office items.
	7 The Convenience Store	Buying things. Polite requests. Inquiries.	*Could? Do you have? I'll.*	Shopping.
	8 Check-in at a Hotel	Asking about vacancies. Checking in. Filling in a form.	Questions. *Would like?* Future simple. *Could?*	Hotel terms. Credit cards.
	9 Hotel Information	Telephoning. Reserving a room. Asking about facilities and prices.	Questions. *Have.* Present simple.	Hotel services and facilities.
	10 Introductions	Formal and informal greetings. Social and personal conversation.	Present continuous. *Going to. If you'll. Will be staying.*	Greetings.
	11 Starting Conversations	Exchanging personal information.	Tenses. Questions. *For. Since. Ago.*	People. Questions.
	12 Ordering Drinks	Ordering in a restaurant.	*Could? Would like.*	Restaurant terms. Drinks.
	13 Lunch	Ordering in a cafeteria.	*There is/was. Have (got).* Present simple.	Food.
	14 A Deli Sandwich	Ordering take-out food. Making choices.	*Would like. Will. Have.* Present simple.	Food.
	15 Flight UA755	Checking in at the airport.	*Have to. Will have to. Should.*	Check-in terms.
	16 Security	Going through airport Security Check.	Imperatives. *Would you mind?* Prepositions.	Security terms.
	17 Traveling Companions	Talking to attendants and other passengers. Apologizing.	Present continuous. *Will have to. Can't.*	In-flight services. Titles.
	18 In Flight	Listening to in-flight announcements.	Tenses. *Have just done. Haven't done yet.*	Air travel terms.

* You can find information about the Grammar items in the 'Grammar Reference Section' in the back of this book.

Business

 Socializing

 Travel

 Hotels

 Money

 Food & Drink

TOPIC	UNIT		COMMUNICATIVE AIMS	GRAMMAR PRACTICE *	VOCABULARY
	19	**Congratulations**	Using and understanding numbers. Paying compliments.	Questions. *Be:* past. Past simple.	Numbers. Math.
	20	**At the Devereux's**	Introductions and greetings in the home. Social conversation at dinner. Manners.	Tenses. *For. Since. Used to.*	Greetings. Food.
	21	**Courtesies**	Thanking someone for dinner. Saying good-bye and apologizing.	*Had better.* Gerunds. Present & Past tenses.	Polite excuses.
	22	**A Trip to the Mall**	Shopping. Discussing consumer goods.	*Have. I'll…* Present tenses.	Colors. Money. Sizes. Clothes.
	23	**At the Post Office**	Sending mail. Filling in a customs form.	*How* + adjectives. *How much/many?*	Weights. Measurements.
	24	**Travelers Checks**	Cashing travelers checks.	*Need. If…*	Currency. Banking terms. Identification.
	25	**Hotel Lobby**	Asking for assistance.	*I'll… Could?*	Transportation. Times.
	26	**Fitness Suite**	Giving directions. Introductions.	*Be:* present. Present perfect. *Ever.* Past simple.	Directions. Greetings. Leisure activities.
	27	**Business Services**	Using secretarial services.	*Want/would like/ something done.* Future simple.	Office tasks. Money.
	28	**Small Talk**	Selecting suitable topics for conversation.	Present and Past tenses. Questions.	General topics for conversation.
	29	**Local Specialties**	Talking about menus and food.	*Would like. Like* + object.	Food. Places.
	30	**On the Phone**	Answering the phone. Asking for confirmation. Making arrangements.	Prepositions.	Alphabet. Times. Places.
	31	**Telephone Facilities**	Making long distance phone calls.	*If* + infinitive.	Telephone. Addresses. Places.
	32	**Duty-Free**	Discussing rules and regulations.	*Allowed to. Can. How much/many?*	Duty-free store items. Measurements. Currency.
	33	**Lost Baggage**	Dealing with problems.	Past simple. *Have you ever?* Verbs and prepositions.	Baggage contents & identification. Places.
	34	**Airport Arrivals**	Going through immigration. Filling in an Arrival form.	Present continuous. *How long?* Questions.	Lengths of time. Personal data.
	35	**Customs**	Going through customs. Filling in a customs declaration form.	*Do you have?*	Customs terms. Personal data.

Business

Socializing

Travel

Hotels

Money

Food & Drink

TOPIC		UNIT	COMMUNICATIVE AIMS	GRAMMAR PRACTICE *	VOCABULARY
	36	**Asking for Directions**	Asking for and giving street directions.	Prepositions. Imperative.	Directions.
	37	**Time Zones**	Telephoning. Talking about time differences. Looking at indirect questions and statements.	Indirect questions. Prepositions.	Times. Places.
	38	**A Job Interview**	Writing a resume. Interview skills.	Questions. Present & Past tenses.	Terms used in job interviews & resumes.
	39	**An Application Form**	Applying for a job. Personal information.	Questions. Present & Past tenses.	Alphabet. Numbers. Dates. Personal data.
	40	**Breakfast in America**	Ordering breakfast.	*I'll... Could?* Passive.	Food.
	41	**Conversations**	Inquiring about family and acquaintances.	Present & Past tenses.	Greetings.
	42	**Describing People**	Giving physical descriptions of people. Location.	*Be. Have.* Prepositions. Present continuous.	Adjectives.
	43	**The Office Party**	Talking about other people. Descriptions continued.	Relative pronoun *who.* Present tenses.	Adjectives.
	44	**A Better Computer**	Comparing things.	Comparatives & Superlatives.	Adjectives.
	45	**Presentations**	Comparing ways of displaying information.	*Should. Need. worth* + gerund.	Numbers. Audio-equipment.
	46	**A Software Brochure**	Ordering from a brochure. Reading for information.	*Need. Can.* Present simple.	Computer software.
	47	**A Market Survey**	Filling out a survey. Letter-writing.	*Which?* Present simple.	Computer software & hardware.
	48	**Talking About Vacations**	Discussing vacations.	Questions. Present & Past tenses.	Types of vacations. Leisure activities.
	49	**Describing Places**	Describing vacations.	Present simple. Past simple. *How?* + adjectives.	Adjectives. Places.
	50	**Reserving an Airline Ticket**	Making a flight reservation.	*Would like.* Present simple.	Dates. Times. Air travel terms.
	51	**Reservations**	Making a restaurant and theater reservation. Filling in a credit card slip.	*Have. I'll...*	Numbers. Times. Theater terms. Restaurant terms.
	52	**Car Rental Information**	Choosing a car to rent. Reading for information.	Questions. Superlatives.	Adjectives. Car rental terms.
	53	**Renting a Car**	Organizing a car rental.	*How long? For. Until. Can.*	Lengths of time. Car rental terms.

* You can find information about all the Grammar items in the 'Grammar Section'. They are listed alphabetically.

Business

Socializing

Travel

Hotels

Money

Food & Drink

TOPIC		UNIT	COMMUNICATIVE AIMS	GRAMMAR PRACTICE *	VOCABULARY
		54	**Driving in the U.S.A.**	Traveling by road. Reading for information.	Modals. Passive.	Driving terms.
		55	**Communications**	Sending business documents.	*Need. Can? Want something done. Want someone to do.*	Mailing terms.
		56	**Medical Problems**	Getting medical help. Filling in a medical form.	Tenses. *How?*	Medical problems. Treatments.
		57	**Hotel Problems**	Confrontations and how to avoid them.	*Can. If…*	Hotel check-in/out terms.
		58	**Complaints**	Complaining about a problem.	Relative pronoun: *who?* Present perfect continuous	Hotel staff & services.
		59	**Guest Comments**	Getting things done. Filling in a form.	*Have something done.* Questions. Tenses.	Adjectives. Facilities.
		60	**Somewhere to Go**	Making suggestions. Planning leisure time. Reading for information.	Gerunds/Infinitive.	Numbers. Places. Times. Addresses.
		61	**Invitations**	Making, accepting and refusing invitations.	Future tenses. *How about?*	Expressions for invitations.
		62	**Agreeing and Disagreeing**	Giving your opinion.	Modals. *So/neither.* Present simple.	Likes & dislikes. Marketing terms.
		63	**Advertising**	Discussing the media and consumers. Reading for information.	Adverbs. Present simple.	The media. Consumer groups & goods.
		64	**Giving Opinions**	Making your point.	*Should.* Comparatives & Superlatives.	Controversial issues.
		65	**Registering at a Convention**	Identifying and registering yourself. Asking and giving directions indoors.	Prepositions. Imperative.	Directions.
		66	**Making Plans**	Organizing people.	*Want someone to do. How long? For.*	Terms used at conventions.
		67	**Preparing a Speech**	Making speeches. Correcting politely.	*How about? Had better.*	Expressions for speeches.
		68	**Convention Planner**	Making choices. Reading a timetable.	*Going to.* Tenses.	Terms used at conventions.
		69	**Room Service**	Ordering a room service meal.	Future simple.	Food.
		70	**Check-Out**	Discussing your hotel bill. Justifying your expenses.	Past simple.	Hotel accounts.
		71	**Survival**	A game to see if you can survive in English!	All grammar.	All vocabulary.
		72	**Good-Bye**	Thanking people and saying good-bye. Keeping in touch.	Gerunds/Infinitive. Future simple.	Expressions for saying good-bye.

Grammar Reference *(Survival Files)*   **Transcript**   **Wordlist**

Introducing Survival English

These are some of the people in Survival English.
There is no story, but you will see these people several times in the book. You'll also meet other people from around the world, all of them surviving successfully in English. Good Luck!

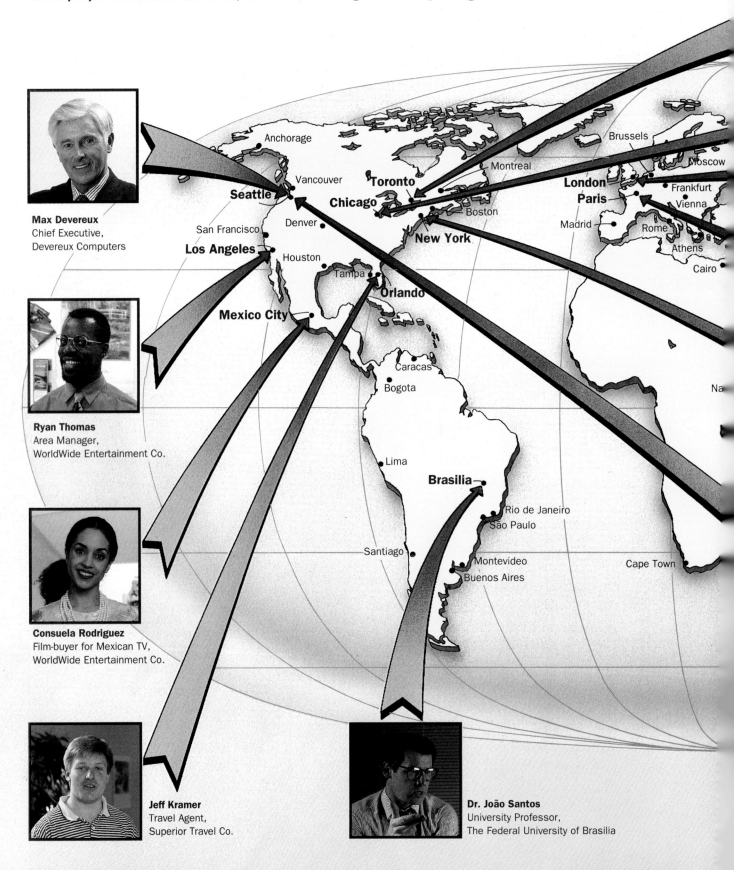

Max Devereux
Chief Executive,
Devereux Computers

Ryan Thomas
Area Manager,
WorldWide Entertainment Co.

Consuela Rodriguez
Film-buyer for Mexican TV,
WorldWide Entertainment Co.

Jeff Kramer
Travel Agent,
Superior Travel Co.

Dr. João Santos
University Professor,
The Federal University of Brasilia

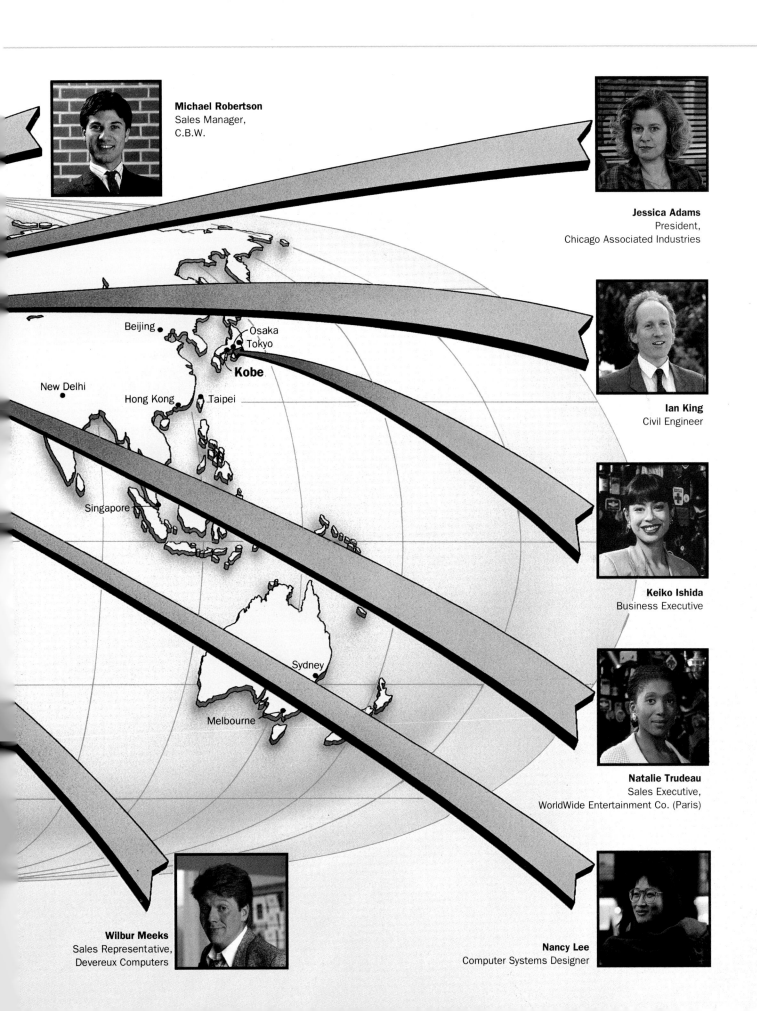

Michael Robertson
Sales Manager,
C.B.W.

Jessica Adams
President,
Chicago Associated Industries

Ian King
Civil Engineer

Keiko Ishida
Business Executive

Natalie Trudeau
Sales Executive,
WorldWide Entertainment Co. (Paris)

Nancy Lee
Computer Systems Designer

Wilbur Meeks
Sales Representative,
Devereux Computers

Beijing

Osaka
Tokyo

Kobe

New Delhi

Hong Kong

Taipei

Singapore

Sydney

Melbourne

Welcome

Welcome to **Survival English**, a practical and exciting course for people who need English for work or travel.

This book is based around real-life situations, and along with the cassettes or CDs, gives you everything you need to survive in English. There's a Practice Book too, if you want more written work.

Every page is easy to use and learn from, and gives you important new language which you can read, listen to, practice, and use. You'll be able to make simple everyday conversations, order meals, change travelers checks, check in to a hotel, have meetings, and much, much more!

You can access the book page by page, or dip into it by using the topic symbols to find the situations and language which you need most.

You'll also find helpful grammar reference in the Survival Files at the back, and for building vocabulary there's a 400-word wordlist with translations in six languages.

Whether you need English for business trips, vacations, or work with English speakers, **Survival English** is right for you!

Index of Topics

Business

2, 3, 4, 5, 6, 10, 19, 23, 27, 30, 31, 37, 38, 39, 44, 45, 46, 47, 51, 55, 63, 64, 65, 66, 67, 68

Socializing

2, 10, 11, 17, 20, 21, 26, 28, 29, 41, 42, 43, 48, 49, 51, 60, 61, 62, 72

Travel

1, 15, 16, 17, 18, 32, 33, 34, 35, 36, 37, 50, 52, 53, 54, 56

Hotels

8, 9, 25, 26, 27, 40, 57, 58, 59, 69, 70

Money

1, 7, 22. 23. 24. 32, 70

Food & Drink

12, 13, 14, 20, 21, 29, 40, 69

1 Taxi!

Ian King has just arrived in Atlanta.

Ian King: Taxi!
Cab Driver: Hi, mister. Where to?
Ian King: The Sheraton, please.
Cab Driver: Which one? There are three Sheratons here in Atlanta.
Ian King: Oh, sorry. The Sheraton Century Center.
Cab Driver: OK, sure. Are you here on business or on vacation?
Ian King: On business.
Cab Driver: Right. Hey, where are you from?
Ian King: England.
Cab Driver: England? Which part?
Ian King: Winchester. Do you know it?
Cab Driver: No. I was in Norfolk when I was in the air force. Nice country.
Ian King: Thanks.

Cab Driver: Well, here we are. This is the Sheraton. That's $7.80.
Ian King: Thank you. Keep the change.
Cab Driver: Hey, mister! This is a five dollar bill!
Ian King: Oh, sorry. I thought it was a ten. There you go.
Cab Driver: Thanks. Have a good stay.

1 Match

a cent
a nickel
a dime
a quarter

Remember! American bills are all the same color and the same size!
The bills in common use are $1, $5, $10, $20, $50, and $100.

Tips

In America, you usually give tips to waiters, bartenders, cab drivers, etc. Tips are a large part of their pay. Think of 20% for most services.
This is a guide:

Waiter – 20%	Bell hop – $1 per bag	Hairdresser – 20%
Cab driver – 20%	Housekeeper – $1 per day	

You don't give tips at gas stations, the movies, or at theaters.

► Do you tip in your country? When do you tip?

2 Match

tip   cab
dollar   room maid
taxi   buck
bell hop   bell person
housekeeper   gratuity

2 Mr. Robertson Arrives

Michael Robertson: Excuse me.
Secretary: Yes?
Michael Robertson: Good morning. My name's Michael Robertson.
Secretary: Good morning, Mr. Robertson. How can I help you?
Michael Robertson: I have an appointment with Ms. Jessica Adams.
Secretary: Ah, yes. Mr. Robertson. Ten fifteen.
Michael Robertson: That's right. Sorry I'm late.
Secretary: That's all right. Will you follow me, please?
Michael Robertson: Thank you.

Jessica Adams: Mr. Robertson? How do you do?
Michael Robertson: Fine, thank you. And you?
Jessica Adams: Oh fine, Mr. Robertson.
Michael Robertson: Please, call me Michael.
Jessica Adams: Right, Michael. And I'm Jessica. So, how was the trip?
Michael Robertson: Well, not too bad. But I'm sorry I'm late. The plane was delayed.
Jessica Adams: That's OK. How was the traffic from the airport?
Michael Robertson: Pretty awful!

There is a knock at the door.
Jessica Adams: Oh, that'll be Dave. Come in. Michael Robertson, this is Dave Scott, our Canadian representative.
Michael Robertson: Nice to meet you, Dave.
Dave Scott: It's nice to meet you too, Michael.
Jessica Adams: Michael is the Sales Manager at C.B.W. in Toronto.
Dave Scott: Sure. I know C.B.W. Is this your first trip to Chicago, Michael?
Michael Robertson: Yes. Yes, it is.
Jessica Adams: Take a seat. I'll phone for some coffee …

1 **Match the greetings with the most likely responses.**

Greeting	Response
How do you do?	Hello.
Good morning.	Good morning.
Good afternoon.	Hi!
Good evening.	Good afternoon.
Hello, there.	Fine, thank you. And you?
Hi!	Good evening.

What is the *general rule* for responses to greetings?

2 **Practice greetings and responses with a partner.**

3 **Look at the conversations and highlight the questions which are useful for "breaking the ice".**

Breaking the ice
North Americans often like to use first names as soon as possible. It's a good way to "break the ice" (begin a conversation in a friendly way).

3 Appointments and Dates

Secretary: Good morning. May I help you?
Michael Robertson: Yes, I have an appointment with Ms. Adams.
Secretary: What time's your appointment?
Michael Robertson: It's at 10:30.

With a partner, make similar conversations about the other people named on the business cards.

HONEYCREST INC.

Andrew Kennedy Jr.
Chief Executive Officer

11:30

10:00

CHICAGO ASSOCIATED INDUSTRIES

CAI

Charles Stevens
Executive Vice-President

3:00

Translation Services

Claire Wilson
Co-ordinator

9:30

Dr. Karen Mendelsohn D.D.S.

JANUARY	FEBRUARY	MARCH	APRIL
S M T W T F S	S M T W T F S	S M T W T F S	S M T W T F S
1 2 ③ 4	1	1 2 3 4 5 6 7	1 2 3 4
5 6 7 8 9 10 11	2 3 4 5 6 7 8	8 9 10 11 12 13 14	5 6 7 8 ⑨ 10 11
12 13 14 15 16 17 18	9 10 11 12 ⑬ 14 15	15 ⑯ 17 18 19 20 21	12 13 14 15 16 17 18
19 20 21 22 23 24 25	16 17 18 19 20 21 22	22 23 24 25 26 27 28	19 20 21 22 23 24 25
26 27 28 29 30 31	23 24 25 26 37 28 29	29 30 31	26 27 28 29 30

MAY	JUNE	JULY	AUGUST
S M T W T F S	S M T W T F S	S M T W T F S	S M T W T F S
① 2	1 2 3 4 5 6	1 2 3 4	1
3 4 5 6 7 8 9	7 8 9 10 11 12 13	5 6 7 8 9 10 11	2 3 4 5 6 7 8
10 11 12 13 14 15 16	14 15 16 17 18 19 20	12 13 14 15 16 17 18	9 10 11 12 13 14 15
17 18 19 20 21 22 23	21 22 23 24 ㉕ 26 27	19 20 21 22 23 24 25	16 ⑰ 18 19 20 21 22
²⁴/₃₁ 25 26 27 28 29 30	28 29 30	26 27 28 29 ㉚ 31	²³/₃₀ ²⁴/₃₁ 25 26 27 28 29

SEPTEMBER	OCTOBER	NOVEMBER	DECEMBER
S M T W T F S	S M T W T F S	S M T W T F S	S M T W T F S
1 2 3 4 5	1 2 3	1 ② 3 4 5 6 7	1 ② 3 4 5
6 7 8 9 10 11 12	4 5 6 7 8 9 10	8 9 10 11 12 13 14	6 7 8 9 10 11 12
13 14 15 16 17 18 19	11 12 13 14 15 16 17	15 16 17 18 19 20 21	13 14 15 16 17 18 19
20 ㉑ 22 23 24 25 26	18 19 20 21 22 23 24	22 23 24 25 26 27 28	20 21 22 23 24 25 26
27 28 29 30	25 26 27 28 29 ㉚ 31	29 30	27 28 29 30 31

1 Look at the calendar and make sentences for February to December.

January's the first month of the year.

2 Michael Robertson travels a lot. He's going to a different country each month. Look at the calendar and make sentences for:

England / Germany / France / Switzerland / Singapore / Hong Kong / Korea / Japan / Canada / Mexico / Brazil / Argentina.
He's going to England in January.

3 Look at the calendar and Exercise 2. When does he have an appointment in:

London / Bonn / Paris / Berne / Singapore City / Kowloon / Seoul / Tokyo / Vancouver / Mexico City / Brasilia / Buenos Aires?
Michael Robertson has an appointment in London on January 3rd.

4 Circle dates on the calendar which are important to you – birthdays, appointments, trips, etc. With a partner ask and answer questions about these dates.

When's your birthday?
What's on December 19th?

4 Arrangements

Look at John Carter's desk calendar and practice this conversation.

Jessica Adams: Hello, is this Mr. Carter?

John Carter: Yes, John Carter speaking.

Jessica Adams: This is Jessica Adams. I'd like to discuss the IBM contract.

John Carter: Yes, of course. When can you come and see me?

Jessica Adams: Is four o'clock on Monday OK?

John Carter: Four o'clock on Monday. Let me see. No, I'm sorry. I'm interviewing a new secretary then.

Jessica Adams: Well, could I come at nine o'clock on Friday?

John Carter: Yes, that'll be fine. I'll see you then.

1. **Look at the desk calendar and the key language (in blue). Make appointments with your partner.**

2. **Next week Jessica is going on a business trip to Japan and Hong Kong. Look at her itinerary. Ask and answer:**

   a Where is Jessica going to be
   on Tuesday?
   on Thursday?
   on Saturday?

   b When is she going to
   leave Hong Kong?
   arrive in Tokyo?
   return to Chicago?

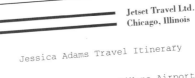

Jetset Travel Ltd.
Chicago, Illinois

Jessica Adams Travel Itinerary

MONDAY:	Chicago, O'Hare Airport Departure: 7:45 a.m.
TUESDAY:	Tokyo, Narita Airport Arrival: 11:00 a.m.
THURSDAY:	Tokyo, Narita Airport Departure: 2:05 p.m. Hong Kong Int'l. Airport Arrival: 4:20 p.m.
FRIDAY:	Hong Kong Int'l Airport Departure: 4:55 p.m.
SATURDAY:	Chicago, O'Hare Airport Arrival: 6:50 a.m.

3. **Discuss:**

   - What arrangements have you made for this week?
   - Do you keep a desk calendar or similar appointment book? Is it well organized?
   - When you travel, are you given an itinerary? Is it useful?

5 What do you do?

Dave Scott: What exactly do you do at C.B.W., Michael?

Michael Robertson: I'm in charge of North American sales. Hey, can I ask you something, Dave?

Dave Scott: Sure. Go ahead.

Michael Robertson: What exactly does Jessica Adams do? I mean, what's her job description?

Dave Scott: That's easy, Michael. She owns the company!

Ask and answer questions about these other people.

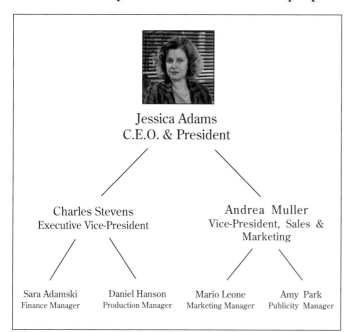

Jessica Adams
C.E.O. & President

Charles Stevens
Executive Vice-President

Andrea Muller
Vice-President, Sales & Marketing

Sara Adamski
Finance Manager

Daniel Hanson
Production Manager

Mario Leone
Marketing Manager

Amy Park
Publicity Manager

1 **Read the information about these famous people. Now, ask and answer these questions:**

Where was he/she born?
When was he/she born?
What nationality is he/she?
Where is he/she from?
What do they do?

2 **Find three people in your class, and ask and answer these questions:**

Where were you born?
When were you born?
What nationality are you?
Where are you from?
What do you do?
Who do you work for?

Princess Diana of Wales
July 1, 1961, Sandringham, England. British

Emperor Akihito
December 23, 1933, Tokyo, Japan. Japanese

Cher
May 20, 1945, El Centro, California. American

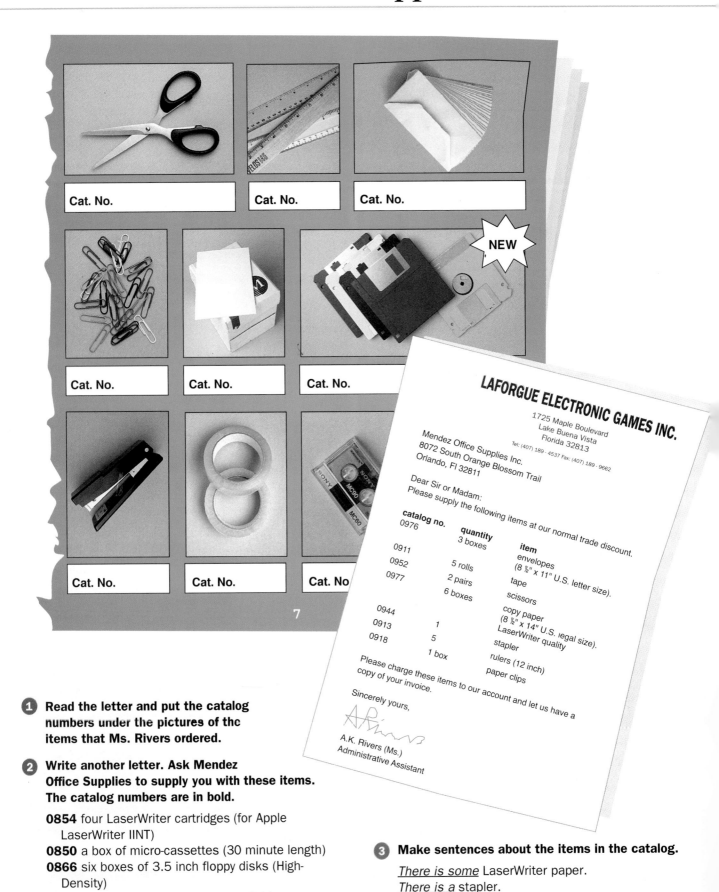

Cat. No.　　　Cat. No.　　　Cat. No.

Cat. No.　　　Cat. No.　　　Cat. No.

NEW

Cat. No.　　　Cat. No.　　　Cat. No

7

LAFORGUE ELECTRONIC GAMES INC.

1725 Maple Boulevard
Lake Buena Vista
Florida 32813
Tel: (407) 189 - 4537 Fax: (407) 189 - 9662

Mendez Office Supplies Inc.
8072 South Orange Blossom Trail
Orlando, Fl 32811

Dear Sir or Madam:
Please supply the following items at our normal trade discount.

catalog no.	quantity	item
0976	3 boxes	
0911		envelopes
0952	5 rolls	(8 ½" x 11" U.S. letter size).
0977	2 pairs	tape
	6 boxes	scissors
0944		copy paper
0913	1	(8 ½" x 14" U.S. legal size).
0918	5	LaserWriter quality
	1 box	stapler
		rulers (12 inch)
		paper clips

Please charge these items to our account and let us have a copy of your invoice.

Sincerely yours,

A.K. Rivers (Ms.)
Administrative Assistant

1 **Read the letter and put the catalog numbers under the pictures of the items that Ms. Rivers ordered.**

2 **Write another letter. Ask Mendez Office Supplies to supply you with these items. The catalog numbers are in bold.**

0854 four LaserWriter cartridges (for Apple LaserWriter IINT)

0850 a box of micro-cassettes (30 minute length)

0866 six boxes of 3.5 inch floppy disks (High-Density)

0821 one bottle of screen cleaning fluid

0988 one box of mailing labels

3 **Make sentences about the items in the catalog.**

There is some LaserWriter paper.
There is a stapler.
There are some envelopes.

7 The Convenience Store

Michael Robertson: Excuse me.
Woman: Hi. Can I help you?
Michael Robertson: Do you have *Newsweek* magazine?
Woman: Yes, it's right over there.
Michael Robertson: Oh, yes, I see it. Could you tell me how much it is?
Woman: It's three dollars. Will there be anything else?
Michael Robertson: Could I have a box of tissues, please?
Woman: There you go. Is that all?
Michael Robertson: I'll take two packs of that gum, too.

Woman: Is that the regular or the sugar-free?
Michael Robertson: The sugar-free. That's all then.
Woman: All right. *Newsweek* magazine, a box of Kleenex tissues, and two packs of gum. That'll be five dollars and eighteen cents, please.
Michael Robertson: There you go.
Woman: Four dollars and eighty-two cents change. Thank you very much.
Michael Robertson: Thanks. Oh, do you have the time?
Woman: Yes, it's quarter after nine.
Michael Robertson: Thanks a lot.
Woman: You're welcome. Bye.

① In pairs, look at the key language (in blue) and ask about these items:

$1.29   95¢

$1.72

$1.29

85¢

70¢

Late-night shopping
In North America many convenience stores and mini-marts are open 24 hours a day, 7 days a week. They sell a wide range of products.

---

② Discuss in pairs:

- Do you have convenience stores in your country?
- What kind of products do they sell?
- In your country, are convenience stores open 24 hours a day, 7 days a week?

When you're giving something to somebody, you can use any combination of the words in the box, right, and the meaning is the same:
Here you go. / There we are. / There we go. / Here you are. etc.

There	you	go.
Here	we	are.

8 Check-in at a Hotel

Consuela Rodriguez is checking in to the Studios Inn Hotel. Read and listen to Conversation A. Then listen again to the second recording. This time the recording only has the voice of the Front Desk Clerk. You take the part of Consuela Rodriguez.

Conversation A

Front Desk Clerk: Good afternoon. Can I help you?

Consuela Rodriguez: Yes. Do you have any vacancies starting tonight?

Front Desk Clerk: Yes, ma'am, we do. How long would you like to stay?

Consuela Rodriguez: For four nights.

Front Desk Clerk: What kind of room would you like?

Consuela Rodriguez: A single, if possible.

Front Desk Clerk: Let me see . . . . Will you be paying by credit card?

Consuela Rodriguez: Yes. MasterCard. Here you are.

Front Desk Clerk: That's Ms. Rodriguez? I'll just take an impression of your card. Would you please complete the guest registration card?

Consuela Rodriguez: Certainly.

Conversation B

Front Desk Clerk: Here's your credit card, Ms. Rodriguez, and your room key.

Consuela Rodriguez: Thank you.

Front Desk Clerk: This is your room charge card. You'll need this if you charge anything in the restaurant or lobby shops. Could you sign it here?

Consuela Rodriguez: OK.

Front Desk Clerk: Right. Your room is on the seventh floor. The bell captain will take your bags up to your room.

Consuela Rodriguez: Thank you. Oh, is the restaurant still serving lunch?

Front Desk Clerk: Our main restaurant closes at two-thirty, but you can get something to eat in the All-Day Coffee Shop. It's located across the lobby.

Consuela Rodriguez: Thank you very much.

Front Desk Clerk: You're very welcome. Enjoy your stay with us.

1 **Interview another student and complete this guest registration card for them.**

Studios Inn Hotel 🏨 Hollywood Boulevard

GUEST REGISTRATION CARD

Last name: _____ First name: _____ Middle initial: _____

Title: _____ Home address: _____

_____ Home phone number: (___) _____

Company name: _____ Company address: _____

_____ Company phone number: (___) _____

Nationality (only for non-U.S. citizens): _____ Passport number: _____

Next Destination: _____ Car License plate: _____ State: _____

2 **Look at Conversation B, and answer these questions:**

a What does the Front Desk Clerk give Consuela?

b What floor is Consuela's room on?

c What time does the main restaurant close?

3 **Discuss:**

• What kind of things do you buy with a credit card? Do you use it for small purchases?

• What are the major credit cards in your country?

• Do you think people will use cash at all in the future?

9 Hotel Information

1 **Listen to the recording of Conversation A. Find these facts:**

a What kind of room does she want?
b How much will the room be per night?

2 **Listen again to Conversation A. Then, with a partner, have a similar conversation asking about hotel room prices.**

3 **In pairs, read Conversation B below and the Studios Inn Price List. Then, ask and answer similar questions with** *Does it have ...? / Do you have ...?*

Conversation B
Consuela Rodriguez is phoning a friend from her room at the Studios Inn.

Consuela Rodriguez: Hi, Karen? This is Consuela.
Karen Paulsen: Consuela! Great to hear from you. Where are you?
Consuela Rodriguez: At the Studios Inn, in Hollywood.
Karen Paulsen: Really? What's it like?
Consuela Rodriguez: Very nice. The room's huge.
Karen Paulsen: Yes? Does it have satellite TV?
Consuela Rodriguez: No, it doesn't, but it has ...

Studios Inn Hotel
Hollywood Boulevard

PRICES

Executive suite (two luxury bedrooms) — $695 per night
Bedroom 1, has king size bed, Bathroom
Bedroom 2, has two queen size beds, Bathroom
plus, connecting parlor with wide screen TV,
Wet bar, Guest Washroom.

Standard suite — $450 per night
Bedroom with king size bed, Bathroom,
Parlor, Wet Bar

Double room (1 or 2 person occupancy)
With king size bed: — $125 per person supplement
With two queen size beds: — $125 per person supplement
(*Children under 14 sharing a room with two adults stay FREE*)

Single room (1 person occupancy) — $170 per night
with one double bed

Extras: — $30 per night
Cot/Rollaway bed (for children under 8)

ALL OUR ROOMS HAVE PRIVATE BATH, SHOWER, DIRECT-DIAL
TELEPHONE, INDIVIDUAL CLIMATE CONTROLS & COLOR TV.

State tax (currently at 18%) will be added to all charges.
Service included. Additional gratuities at your discretion.

---

4 **Look at Conversation C, below. Complete the sentences, then listen to the recording and compare.**

Conversation C

Front Desk Clerk: What kind of room ....?

You: I'd like a ....

Front Desk Clerk: Fine. I have a ....
....

You: Does it have ....?

Front Desk Clerk: No, it doesn't. It has a
....

You: That's OK.

Front Desk Clerk: How are you paying?

You: ....

Hotel facilities
Large hotels usually prefer payment by credit card, and you can assume that rooms will have facilities like a bathroom, color TV, and direct-dial telephone. In small hotels you may have to ask about things like these:
Room Service / Sports Room / Business Services / Pool / Air Conditioning / Jacuzzi / Non-Smoking Rooms / Hair Dryer / Color TV / Satellite TV / Telephone / Fax Machine.

10 Introduction

Conversation A
Michael Robertson has arrived for another meeting.

Jessica Adams: Michael! Come in, come in. I'd like you to meet Josh Crosby.
Josh Crosby: How do you do, Michael?
Michael Robertson: I'm very well, thank you. It's nice to meet you.
Jessica Adams: Josh is our company lawyer. He's taking care of the contracts.
Michael Robertson: I see.
Josh Crosby: I hear you're from Canada.
Michael Robertson: Yes, that's right.
Josh Crosby: How long will you be staying in the States?
Michael Robertson: Oh, about three months.
Josh Crosby: How do you like it here so far?
Michael Robertson: It's great. Really enjoying it.
Josh Crosby: Well, if you'll excuse me, I have to go. It was nice meeting you.
Michael Robertson: Thanks, nice meeting you, too. Hope to see you again sometime.

Conversation B
Michael met Josh several more times. Here they meet each other on the street.

Josh Crosby: Michael!
Michael Robertson: Josh!
Josh Crosby: Hi. How are you?
Michael Robertson: I'm well thanks. And you?
Josh Crosby: Oh, I'm fine. How's Jodie?
Michael Robertson: She's fine, too.
Josh Crosby: Good.
Michael Robertson: She's really enjoying Chicago.
Josh Crosby: Lousy weather, though.
Michael Robertson: Well, it's the same up in Toronto.
Josh Crosby: Yeah. Listen, I have to be off. I'm already late - but it was good seeing you again, Mike.
Michael Robertson: Yeah, good to see you, too. Bye. Take care.

1 **Look at the key expressions (in blue).**
Can you replace them with different expressions below?

Conversation A
I want to introduce …
Please meet …
This is …
May I introduce you to …
Pleased to meet you.
How long are you going to be here?
How long are you staying here?
Hope to meet you again.
It was a pleasure to meet you.

Conversation B
I've got to go.
Look after yourself.
See you later.
I'm fine, thanks.
Not too bad, thanks.
I've got to be going.
I'd better be going.
Keep well.

2 **In threes, practice introductions.**

3 **Discuss in threes:**

How do you introduce / greet / say good-bye to friends / business people in your country and in other countries?

11 Starting Conversations

The best way to begin a conversation is to ask questions.

Question		Response
Where are you from? *Where do you come from?*		*I'm from (Canada).* *I come from (Canada).*
How long have you been here? *When did you get here?*		*I've been here since (January).* *I've been here for (three days).* *I got here (two days ago).*
How long are you staying? *How long will you be staying?* *How long are you going to stay?*		*Until next (Sunday).* *For another (five days).*
How do you like it here? *What do you think of (Chicago)?* *How are you finding (Chicago)?*		*It's very (nice / interesting).* *I like it (very much / a lot).*
What are you here for? *Are you here on (business)?* *Why are you here?*		*I'm (visiting customers).* *I'm (buying equipment).* *I'm here (for the convention).*

Monique Flaubert is from Quebec. She's just met Marcia Hurley from Jamaica at a conference.

Carlos Alberto Ramos is from Brazil. Krystyna Kowalski is from Poland. They're both working in the United States.

1 **In pairs. Look at the people in the photographs.**

Student A: Choose one person from each of the photographs. Look at the questions in the box. Write facts about the person which will answer the questions.

Student B: Do the same for the other person in each of the pictures. Don't show your list of facts to your partner.

2 **Use your list of facts and ask and answer questions for each of the pictures.**

3 **Invent a character. Write a list of facts about them in the same way.**

4 **Imagine you are that character. Circulate around the class and introduce yourself to others. Ask them questions about themselves. Answer questions about your imaginary character.**

12 Ordering Drinks

Conversation A

Manager: Good afternoon, ma'am. Do you have a reservation?

Jessica Adams: No, I don't. But, I'd like a table for one, please.

Manager: Smoking or non-smoking?

Jessica Adams: Non-smoking, please.

Manager: Right this way, ma'am. Your waiter will be with you in just one moment.

Jessica Adams: Thank you.

Conversation B

Waiter: Good afternoon, ma'am. I'm Stefan, and I'm your waiter for today. Would you like a drink while you're looking at the menu?

Jessica Adams: Yes, please. Could I see the wine list?

Waiter: Certainly, ma'am. Here you are.

Jessica Adams: Could I have the California Blush?

Waiter: Yes, ma'am. A glass or half a carafe?

Jessica Adams: Just a glass, please.

Waiter: Right away, ma'am.

Jessica Adams: Oh, and could I also have a glass of ice water?

Waiter: Yes certainly. I'll bring it right away.

Jessica Adams: Thank you.

Waiter: You're welcome.

1. **In pairs, ask and answer questions about the wines on the list:** *Where is it from? How much is it? Is it sold by the glass / carafe / bottle ...?*

2. **In pairs, look again at Conversation B. Using the key language (in blue) and the wine list, order drinks in a restaurant.**

3. **Make a list of countries that produce wine. Compare your list with a partner.**

   Does your country produce wine? Which wine would you recommend? Why?

PARK TOWERS HOTEL
WINE LIST

HOUSE WINES	glass (6oz)	half-carafe (1/2 liter)	carafe (1 liter)
Red: California Cabernet Sauvignon	$2.50	$6.50	$12.00
White: California Chablis	$2.50	$6.50	$12.00
Rosé: California Blush	$2.50	$6.50	$12.00

ESTATE BOTTLED WINES	bottle	half-bottle
Red		
Jekel Vineyard Zinfandel (California)	$28.00	-
Rosemount Estate Shiraz (Australia)	$24.00	$16.00
Santo Tomas Cabernet Sauvignon (Mexico)	$24.00	-
White		
Columbia Semillon (Washington State)	$27.00	$15.50
Inniskillen Chardonnay (Canada)	$22.00	$14.00
Canepa Estate Riesling (Chile)	$22.00	-

CHAMPAGNE/SPARKLING		
Moët & Chandon Champagne (France)	$60.00	$35.00
Great Western Champagne-method (New York)	$19.00	$12.00

MINERAL WATERS	
Imported Perrier or Evian water (France)	$6.50
(Perrier available with lemon, lime or berry flavor)	
North Carolina Mountain Spring Water	$4.00
Clearly Canadian (with peach or berry flavor)	$3.50 (small bottle)

13 Lunch

Counter Help: Hi. What can I get for you?

Jeff Kramer: Is there any fish?

Counter Help: There was, but it's all gone.

Jeff Kramer: No fish! Well, what else do you have?

Counter Help: There's some fried chicken. It's Today's Special.

Jeff Kramer: Sounds good.

Counter Help: One Special!

Voice: One Special coming right up!

Jeff Kramer: Got any green beans?

Counter Help: Sure do. Nice and fresh. Do you want mashed potatoes or french fries?

Jeff Kramer: I'll take mashed potatoes.

Counter Help: Do you want a roll with your meal?

Jeff Kramer: Sure. Thanks.

Counter Help: Help yourself to butter or margarine. The ketchup's over there.

Jeff Kramer: Is there any pecan pie?

Counter Help: Sorry. There's none left. We've got some ice-cream.

Jeff Kramer: No, thanks. This is fine.

THE RUNWAY LOUNGE

MENU June 13

Appetizers:
~~Tomato soup~~
Parma ham with melon
Florida Cocktail (orange & grapefruit)
****

Today's Specials:
Country-fried chicken
~~Fresh sea fish~~
served with a selection of vegetables from
the counter or green salad
****

Vegetarian Dishes:
Penne pasta & beans
Oriental stir-fried vegetables & rice
****

Hawaiian Pizza (ham & pineapple)
Salad bar
****

~~Pecan Pie~~
Ice cream (vanilla, chocoalte, strawberry)
Fresh fruit

1 Look at the menu and order your own meal.

2 Sort these foods correctly, by putting a check (✓) in the correct box.

A = **A**ppetizer (served before the main dish)
E = **E**ntree (main dish of the meal)
D = **D**essert (a sweet course at the end of a meal)

A E D
☐ ☐ ☐ Banana Split
☐ ☐ ☐ Caesar Salad
☐ ☐ ☐ Raspberry Sherbet
☐ ☐ ☐ Shrimp Cocktail
☐ ☐ ☐ Sirloin Steak
☐ ☐ ☐ Grilled Chicken

A E D
☐ ☐ ☐ Spicy Chicken Wings
☐ ☐ ☐ Club Sandwich
☐ ☐ ☐ Pâté
☐ ☐ ☐ Spaghetti
☐ ☐ ☐ Tropical Fruit Salad
☐ ☐ ☐ Cream of Mushroom Soup

3 What do you eat at lunch time? Describe your lunch to your partner. Whose lunch do you prefer? Describe your ideal lunch.

14 A Deli Sandwich

Nancy Lee is buying her lunch from a deli (delicatessen). Read the conversation and complete the sentences with your own ideas.

Nancy Lee: Hi, ... corned beef sandwich, please.

Counter Help: .... that be on white, rye, or whole wheat bread?

Nancy Lee: .... whole wheat, please.

Counter Help: .... ketchup, mayonnaise, or mustard?

Nancy Lee: .... mustard, please.

Counter Help: .... be hot or regular?

Nancy Lee: ....

Counter Help: .... lettuce or cabbage on that?

Nancy Lee: ....

Counter Help: .... romaine, endive, radicchio, or ordinary lettuce.

Nancy Lee: .... romaine.

Counter Help: All right. Coming right up!

Nancy Lee: Thank you.

Counter Help: .... anything else with that?

Nancy Lee: Ah, ... small coleslaw and a bag of potato chips.

Counter Help: .... regular potato chips, chili flavor, blue cheese flavor...?

Nancy Lee: Regular. And could I have a dill pickle?

Counter Help: ...., ma'am.

Nancy Lee: Great.

Counter Help: .... $3.95 altogether.

Nancy Lee: There you go.

Counter Help: Out of five. Thank you very much.

Nancy Lee: Thanks. Oh, I forgot. .... a coffee, too.

Counter Help: OK. We have regular coffee, Colombian special blend, Brazilian, Kenyan, Java, expresso, cappuccino or decaffeinated. The decaffeinated comes in regular, Colombian, or expresso only. You can have that with milk, cream, or low-fat creamer. And we have white sugar, brown sugar, unrefined Barbados sugar, or Sweet 'n Low. We have five sizes. Medium, large, extra large, incredibly large, or you can just take the jumbo king-size!

① **Listen to the recording and compare it with your ideas.**

a Were your sentences longer or shorter than the ones on the recording?

b Were your sentences more or less polite?

② **In pairs, make similar conversations at a deli. Order a sandwich of your own choice.**

Enquiring about wants	Asking for things
Do you want ...?	I want ...
Will that be ...?	I'd like ...
Would you like ...?	Can I have ...?
	Could I have ...?
	May I have ...?

③ **Choices, choices, choices! Do you eat burgers? How many different kinds can you buy? What about cheese? Pickles? Onions? Fishburgers? Chickenburgers?**

In pairs, try to order a burger. Try to confuse each other with the choices!

15 Flight UA755

Jeff Kramer is flying to Denver. He's at the check-in desk now.

Check-in clerk: Your ticket, please, sir.

Jeff: There you go.

Check-in clerk: Flight UA755 to Denver, then you're going on to Aspen, on flight RM002?

Jeff: That's right.

Check-in clerk: Do you have any baggage to check, Mr. Kramer?

Jeff: Yes, I do. Just one piece.

Check-in clerk: And did you pack it yourself, Mr. Kramer?

Jeff: Yes, I did.

Check-in clerk: Are any of the articles on this list in your bag?

Jeff: Um… No.

Check-in clerk: Would you like me to tag this bag through to Aspen? Then you won't have to pick it up in Denver.

Jeff: That would be great. Thanks.

Check-in clerk: Do you have a seating preference, Mr. Kramer?

Jeff: An aisle seat. Extra legroom, if possible.

Check-in clerk: Yes, I have a seat next to the emergency exit. So that's Flight UA755 to Denver, departing at 5:30 p.m., boarding at Gate Number 2 in 20 minutes. The flight's scheduled to depart on time. Here's your boarding pass. You'll have to report to the Transfer Desk in Denver for a seat assignment on your connecting flight.

Jeff: Thank you.

Check-in clerk: You're welcome. Have a good flight.

1 **Look at the Restricted Articles Card. Answer true (✓) or false (✗)?**

a ☐ You shouldn't pack an electric razor in your baggage.

b ☐ You shouldn't pack a gun in your baggage.

c ☐ You should carry matches only in hand baggage.

d ☐ You shouldn't pack pens in your baggage.

Restricted Articles

For your safety and the saftey of your fellow passengers, the articles listed below must not be carried in checked baggage:

● Radios, personal stereos, portable computers

● Firearms ● Electrical appliances

● Matches, lighters, or fireworks

FLIGHT DEPARTURES				
Flight #	Destination	Time	Gate #	Information
AC171	**TORONTO**	**3:45**	**11**	**DELAYED - 6:30 pm**
BA421	**LONDON**	**5:15**	**23**	**CLOSED**
AA322	**CHICAGO**	**5:30**	**17**	**LAST CALL**
UA755	**DENVER**	**5:30**	**2**	**NOW BOARDING**
AM591	**MEXICO CITY**	**5:40**	**6**	**NOW BOARDING**
UA632	**SAN FRANCISCO**	**5:45**	**10**	**WAIT IN LOUNGE**
AA186	**BOSTON**	**6:00**	**15**	**WAIT IN LOUNGE**
UA409	**LOS ANGELES**	**6:00**	**-**	**DELAYED 60 MINS**
AA299	**HOUSTON**	**6:10**	**23**	**WAIT IN LOUNGE**
VV201	**LONDON**	**6:15**	**8**	**WAIT IN LOUNGE**

2 **Look at the Departures Board and the key language (in blue). Make similar conversations.**

3 **List the airlines you have flown, on business and vacation. Compare your list with a partner. Which airline has the best check-in service? Why?**

16 Security

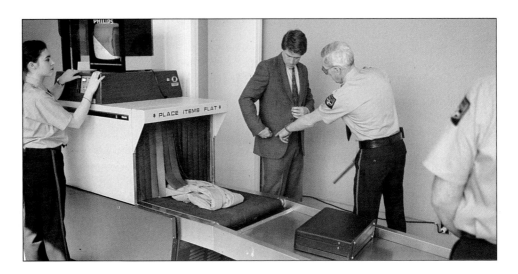

Jeff Kramer is going through the Security Check.

Security: Please put all carry-on luggage on the conveyor … Please put all carry-on luggage on the conveyor. Step right this way, ma'am. This way, sir. (*Beep*) Please empty your pockets and go through again, sir. (*Beep*) Please step this way, sir. Pardon me, what do you have in this pocket?

Jeff: Oh sorry, just some keys.

Security: That's fine. Thank you, sir. Please put all carry-on luggage on the conveyor. Step right this way …

Woman: Is this machine film-safe?

Security: Yes, it is, ma'am. Please put all …

Woman: Are you sure? They're pictures of my granddaughter's first birthday …

Security: You can give the camera to me, ma'am. It doesn't have to go through the scanner. Please put all carry-on luggage on the conveyor. Step right this way …

Jeff goes to pick up his briefcase.

Security (2): Would you mind opening your briefcase, sir?

Jeff: No, not at all … there you go.

Security (2): Would you mind turning on the Walkman?

Jeff: Oh, sorry.

Security: That's fine, sir. We just have to check. You can go through.

① **Fill in the Security Survey. With a partner, compare and discuss your answers.**

② **Using the Wordlist (at the back of this book) or a dictionary, find the meaning in your language, for the words highlighted.**

③ **Discuss:**

- Why do you think Security asked Jeff to turn on his Walkman?
- Why was the woman worried about her camera?
- Why did the scanner "beep" when Jeff went through it? What other items might it detect?

Airport Security Survey

How do you feel about airport security? Check (✔) the boxes.

1. When you are at an airport, what do you prefer?
   ☐ Some security checks ☐ Very careful security checks ☐ No security checks

2. Do you mind opening your carry-on luggage?
   ☐ No, I don't mind ☐ Yes, I do mind

3. Do you mind when they ask you questions?
   ☐ Not at all ☐ Not if they are polite ☐ Yes

4. Do you mind when they search you after you have walked through the scanner?
   ☐ No ☐ Yes

5. How do you feel about airport security staff? (You can check more than one box.)
   ☐ They're doing a difficult but important job. I wouldn't like to do it.
   ☐ I don't like it when they're talking to each other instead of looking at the x-ray scanner.
   ☐ Why do they always stop me?
   ☐ I think they could be more polite.

Conversation A
Jeff Kramer is looking for his seat on the plane.

Jeff: Excuse me. I think I'm in 15C.
Woman: This is 14C.
Jeff: Are you sure?
Woman: Yes, look here ... oh, dear! I am sorry.
Jeff: That's OK. Sorry to disturb you.
Woman: That's quite all right. It's entirely my fault.

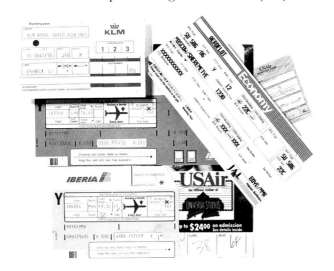

Conversation B

Attendant: Would you like a newspaper, sir?
Jeff: Yes, please ... uh, *USA Today*.
Attendant: I'm afraid we're out of *USA Today*.
  Would you like a *Miami Tribune*?
Jeff: Yes, that's fine.
Attendant: How about you, sir?
Man: Can you get me a Denver
  newspaper?
Attendant: Sure.

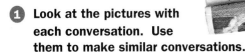

❶ Look at the pictures with each conversation. Use them to make similar conversations.

❷ Look at the key language (in blue) and the Titles below. Role- play conversations with similar "mistakes"!

Titles

General	Academic	Political	Military
Mr.	Professor	President	General
Ms.	Doctor	Senator	Colonel
Mrs.		Governor	Major
Miss	**Medical**	Mayor	Captain
	Doctor		Lieutenant
			Sergeant

Conversation C

Jeff: Excuse me, I didn't get a headset ...
Attendant: Oh, sorry about that. I'll get you one.
Jeff: Thank you.

Conversation D

Man: Are you staying in Denver?
Jeff: No. I'm changing planes there, and going on
  to Aspen. Isn't there a big political convention in
  Denver this week?
Man: Yes, I guess that's why the flight is full. Full of
  politicians, probably.
Jeff: Yeah, I can't stand politicians. They're all
  crooks!
Attendant: Here's the newspaper you wanted,
  Senator.
Man: Thank you.
Jeff: "Senator?" I really am very sorry. I didn't
  mean ...
Man: Don't worry about it! No offence!

❸ A flight attendant on the plane is asking people to obey the regulations. Match the attendant's sentences to the situations.

Situation	Attendant's sentences
1 Someone is smoking a cigar.	**A** I'm sorry, you'll have to turn it off.
2 Someone is using a portable phone.	**B** I'm sorry, you'll have to put it out.
3 Someone is asking about using a Walkman.	**C** I'm afraid you can't use that here.
4 A child is playing an electronic game.	**D** Yes, that's all right.

18 In Flight

Jeff Kramer has to change planes in Denver. Listen to the announcements during his flight to Denver.

Announcement 1

Listen, and check (✓) the correct boxes.

a ☐ They're on a Boeing 767.
☐ They're on a Boeing 747.

b ☐ They have just taken off.
☐ They haven't taken off yet.

c ☐ They can't smoke at the moment.
☐ They can't smoke at all during the flight.

Announcement 2

Listen, and check (✓) the correct boxes.

a ☐ They have just taken off.
☐ They haven't taken off yet.

b ☐ Mr. Kramer must be worried about his connection.
☐ Mr. Kramer has nothing to worry about.

Announcement 3

Are these statements true (✓) or false (✗)?

a ☐ They have only just taken off.
b ☐ They took off several minutes ago.
c ☐ The passengers must not take off their seat belts.
d ☐ The passengers will have lunch in a few hours.
e ☐ The pilot hopes they'll be less than 30 minutes late.

Announcement 4

Answer the questions:

a What is the time now?
b What do the letters E.T.A. stand for?
c What is their E.T.A. in Denver?
d What is the temperature in Denver?
e Is Mr. Kramer still worried about his connection?
f How late will the plane be arriving in Denver?

Announcement 5

Are these statements true (✓) or false (✗)?

a ☐ They haven't landed yet.
b ☐ They have just landed.
c ☐ Mr. Kramer has 45 minutes before his connecting flight.

SUPERIOR TRAVEL

Travel Itinerary   Mr. J.M. Kramer

TRAVELING TO: ASPEN, COLORADO

Please report to the airport one hour before departure.

1) United Airlines Flight UA755 to Denver/Stapleton
Depart: Orlando, 5:30 p.m. Eastern Time
Arrive: Denver, 7:18 p.m. Mountain Time

TRANSFER TO:

Please report to the transfer desk immediately upon arrival in Denver.

2) Rocky Mountain Air, Flight RM002 to Aspen
Depart: Denver, 8:15 p.m.
Arrive: Aspen, 8:40 p.m.

THESE TICKETS ARE NON-TRANSFERABLE

19 Congratulations!

1 Wilbur Meeks is a sales representative. Last week he signed a contract with Burlingham Inc. He wrote a report for the Chief Executive of his company. Yesterday the Chief Executive asked to see him. Listen to the recording, then answer questions a–h in the box.

> **a** Whose office was it?
> ....
>
> **b** Was the Chief Executive angry?
> ....
>
> **c** Why was Wilbur Meeks surprised?
> ....
>
> **d** What was the Chief Executive happy about?
> ....
>
> **e** Did he know Wilbur well?
> ....
>
> **f** Was the contract worth $100,000?
> ....
>
> **g** How much was it worth?
> ....
>
> **h** What was the mistake in Wilbur Meeks's report?
> ....

2 Say these figures out loud:

5,000.00	5,000,000
500,000	500,000.00
500.00	5 000.00
5 000 000	5.053
50,000.00	

Note: When typing, you usually use a comma (,) or sometimes a blank space, to separate the thousands. A period (.) is used for decimals (0.5), and therefore to separate dollars and cents (or pounds and pence etc.).

3 Draw a line to match the figures with the words.

314692	Three hundred and fourteen, point six nine two
314,692	Three, one, four, six, nine, two
314.692	Three hundred and fourteen thousand, six hundred and ninety-two

4 Look at these figures. Say them out loud, and then write them out in full.

a 10,000 ....

b 4.5 ....

c 6 !s ....

d 3% ....

e 56.67 ....

f 32°F ....

g 6,500,253 ....

h $4.07 ....

i 0°C ....

j 10 ÷ 2 = 5 ....

k 3 + 3 − 6 = 0 ....

....

20 At the Devereux's

It's Sunday evening. Wilbur and Charlene Meeks have just arrived at Max and Helena Devereux's house for dinner. Max Devereux is Wilbur's boss.

Conversation A

Helena: Why, hello. You must be Mr. and Mrs. Meeks. Please come in. My husband's told me so much about you.

Charlene: Nothing bad, I hope.

Helena: Ha, ha. Ah… no, of course not. Let me take your coats.

Charlene: Thank you, Mrs. Devereux.

Helena: Please, call me Helena, dear.

Charlene: Thank you, Helena. My name's Charlene … and this is Wilbur.

Conversation B

Helena: How long have you been living in Seattle?

Charlene: Only three weeks. We love it here.

Wilbur: Yes. I used to work in the London office, then in Boston. I still travel to Boston once or twice a month.

Helena: Oh, by the way, Max is in the kitchen. He's cooking dinner tonight. He always cooks a special roast dinner when we have guests.

Wilbur: Oh, good. We just love meat. Don't we, Charlene?

Charlene: Um…Yes, yes, we do.

Conversation C

Max: Fine. Dinner's ready. Would you like to sit over there, Charlene?

Charlene: Thank you.

Max: And perhaps you'd like to sit right here, Wilbur.

Wilbur: Thank you so much, sir … I mean, Mr. Devereux … I mean Max.

Max: Great. Help yourselves to salad. I'll get the plates …

Conversation D

Max: There we go. Could you pass this plate down to Charlene, Wilbur?

Wilbur: Sure. Mmm. Smells good.

Max: Oh, and could you pass me the salt and pepper?

Wilbur: There you are.

Max: Good. Well, to your very good health! Cheers! Enjoy your meal!

---

1 **Have similar conversations. Try to replace the key phrases (in blue) with the words and expressions below.**

Conversation A
I've heard a lot about you.
Max has spoken of you often.
Can I take your coats?
May I take your coats?

Conversation B
Not very long.
Since February.
For a couple of months.
I used to work in New York.
I used to live in New England.

Conversation C
Wilbur, you sit over there.
Charlene, perhaps you could sit next to me.
Please help yourselves to salad / bread / salad dressing.

Conversation D
Could you pass the bread / wine / salad / ketchup?
Bon appetit / Enjoy!

2 **Organize your class for a dinner party. Greet each other. Take coats. Get everyone to sit in the right places. Now move them around, politely, in English!**

Etiquette

There are many different "unwritten rules" about eating and drinking. They are different in different countries. These are some "rules" which are common in the U.S.A.

Don't put your elbows on the table.

Always serve women with food before men.

Always serve guests first.

To cut up food, hold your knife in the right hand and your fork in the left.

When you eat soup, move the spoon away from you.

Don't speak with your mouth full.

21 Courtesies

Wilbur and Charlene Meeks have just had dinner with Wilbur's boss.

Wilbur: Well, ¹I think we'd better be going. It's almost ten-thirty.

Helena: Is that really the time? Time flies when you're enjoying yourself. Um, I hope you had a good time.

Wilbur: Yes, we have. ²Thank you for inviting us.

Charlene: We've had a really wonderful evening.

Helena: ³I'm glad you enjoyed yourselves.

Charlene: Oh, yes, we have. It was a delicious meal.

Helena: Thank you.

Wilbur: I am sorry about the carpet. I hope you can get it clean.

Helena: I'm sure we can.

Charlene: I hope I didn't offend you. It's a very nice fur coat ... it's just that, well, I think it's wrong to kill little animals for fur, you know.

Helena: Uh huh. You told me.

Wilbur: Anyway, our cab should be here any minute.

Charlene: ⁴Next time, you'll have to come over to our place for dinner.

Helena: Thank you.

Wilbur: I think I hear our cab now. Please thank Mr. Devereux ... I mean, Max ... for us ...

Charlene: ... when he wakes up, that is.

Helena: Of course I will. Uh, I'm very sorry that Max fell asleep ...

① **Have a similar conversation, and replace the key phrases (in blue) with the ones in the boxes below.**

1

| We have to go now.
We'd better go now.
It's time we were going.
It's time for us to leave. |

3

| Thank you for coming!
It was a pleasure having you.
Don't mention it.
You're welcome. |

2

| Thank you for a nice evening.
I really enjoyed it!
Thanks for dinner!
Thanks for having us!
I haven't enjoyed myself so much for a long time!
It was a wonderful evening! |

4

| It's our turn next time.
I hope you can join us for dinner next time.
We should do this again. |

② **With a partner. List polite excuses for leaving a social event early. Use these in a conversation, and remember to thank your host!**

③ **Discuss:**

- Why did Wilbur apologize?
- What do you think Charlene said about fur coats?
- Why do you think Max fell asleep?

22 A Trip to the Mall

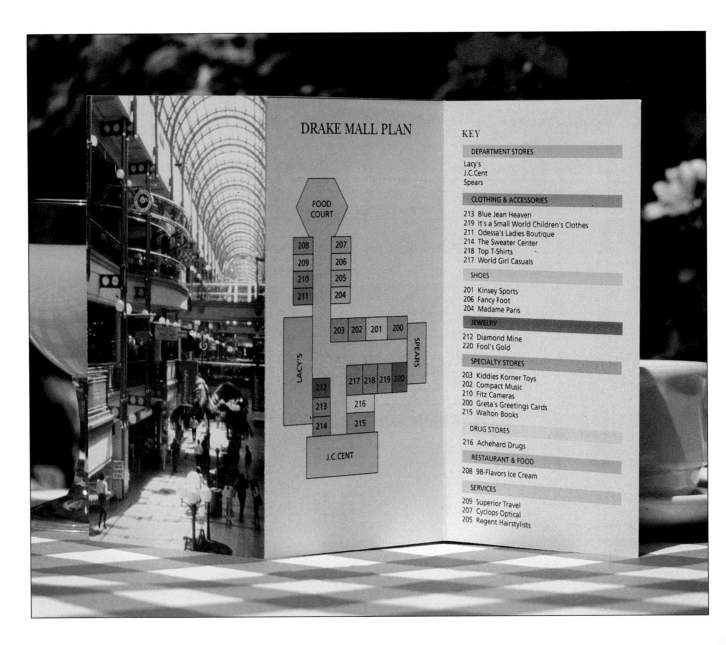

1 Consuela Rodriguez is in Los Angeles on business. She has some spare time on her first morning, and she has come to the Drake Mall to do some shopping. Listen to the four conversations, then listen again and complete the chart.

Note: You might not be sure about the stores, but you can guess!

Conversation	Which store was she in?	What did she buy?	Who was it for?	How much did she spend?
1				
2				
3				
4				

2 What do you think you can buy at the stores in the Drake Mall? Ask and answer in pairs.

3 Now look at the transcripts in the back of this book. Make similar conversations.

4 Make notes about shopping in your country, under the headings below. Then, compare your notes with others.

- opening hours
- types of stores you visit
- how often you shop

1 **Listen to the recording of Consuela Rodriguez in the post office. Take notes and then fill in the form as she did.**

CUSTOMS – DOUANE C1
May be officially opened
(peut être ouvert d'office)

Business papers: .... ☐ ☐
yes   no

Contents in detail:

Désignation detaillée du contenu:

_____

_____

_____

_____

Mark X here if a gift:

Il s'agit d'un cadeau: .... ☐

or a sample of merchandise:

d'un échantillon de marchandises: .... ☐

Value/Valeur: _____

Weight/Poids: _____

Your item must not contain any dangerous articles prohibited by postal regulations.

---

2 **Student A:** It's 36˚ Fahrenheit.
Student B: Really? How much is that in Celsius?
Student A: About two degrees Celsius.

Use this information and make similar conversations.

a He's 6 feet tall. (1.8 meters)
b It's 60 miles away. (100 kilometers)
c There are 4 gallons of gas in the car. (17 liters)
d There are 2 pints of water. (about 1 liter)
e She weighs about 180 pounds. (80 kilograms)

3 **Match. Then put a check (✔) beside the words which are metric.**

ft.   inch
in.   mile
yd.   meter ✔
mi.   gallon
m   kilometer
kg.   yard
gal.   kilogram
qt.   quart
km   feet
l   liter
lb.   pound

Conversion Chart: U.S. / Metric
1 inch = 25 millimeters
1 foot = 30 centimeters
1 yard = 90 centimeters
1 mile = 1.6 kilometers
1 ounce = 28 grams
1 pound = 0.454 kilograms
1 liter = 1.76 pints (U.K.)/2.1 pints (U.S.)*
1 gallon = 4.5 liters (U.K.)/ 4 liters (U.S.)*
100°C = 212°F
0°C = 32°F
* Note: A U.S. and a U.K. *pint* and *gallon* are different measures.

Measurements
The U.S.A. does not generally use the metric system. But, Europe, Canada and Mexico do.

Spelling note: The endings of metric measures are written as *-er* in the U.S., but as *-re* in the U.K.: liter/litre, meter/metre.

24 Travelers Checks

Ian King has come from Britain to supervise a job at a manufacturing plant in Atlanta. He's at his hotel.

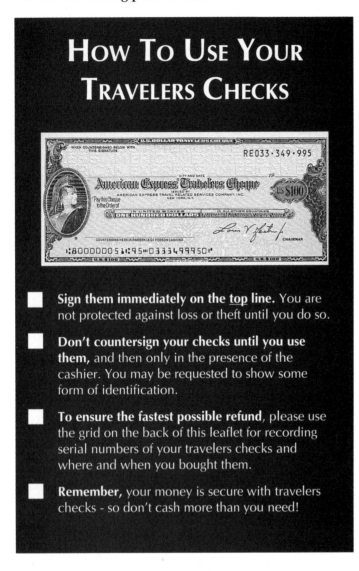

HOW TO USE YOUR TRAVELERS CHECKS

☐ **Sign them immediately on the <u>top</u> line.** You are not protected against loss or theft until you do so.

☐ **Don't countersign your checks until you use them,** and then only in the presence of the cashier. You may be requested to show some form of identification.

☐ **To ensure the fastest possible refund**, please use the grid on the back of this leaflet for recording serial numbers of your travelers checks and where and when you bought them.

☐ **Remember,** your money is secure with travelers checks - so don't cash more than you need!

Cashier: Good morning, Mr. King. What can I do for you today?

Ian King: I'd like to change some travelers checks.

Cashier: All right sir, how much money would you like?

Ian King: Five hundred dollars.

Cashier: Oh, I see. They're American Express dollar travelers checks.

Ian King: Yes. Is that a problem?

Cashier: No problem, sir. It's just that you don't need to change them.

Ian King: I don't understand.

Cashier: Here in the United States, you can use them in stores, just like cash.

Ian King: But I'll need some small bills.

Cashier: Yes, but if you buy something that's ten dollars, and you pay with a fifty dollar travelers check, you'll get the change in cash.

Ian King: Really?

Cashier: Oh, yes, and it's safer not to carry around too much cash. Why don't you just cash a hundred dollars for now?

Ian King: OK. A hundred dollars.

Cashier: Sign here, write the name of the city and the date on both checks.

Ian King: There you go. Ian King, Atlanta, 13.7.

Cashier: Excuse me, Mr. King. Here in the States we don't write the date that way. We write the month then the day, so it's 7.13. Now, may I see some identification? It's hotel policy.

Ian King: I have my passport, or a driver's license, or a credit card.

Cashier: That's fine. One hundred dollars. Here you are. Have a nice day.

---

1 Look at today's newspaper, and write in the equivalents in your currency.

CURRENCY EXCHANGE

- 🏴 G.B. Pound _____
- 🇺🇸 U.S. Dollar _____
- 🇨🇦 Canadian Dollar _____
- 🇫🇷 French Franc _____
- 🇨🇭 Swiss Franc _____
- German Mark _____
- 🇯🇵 Japanese Yen _____
- Spanish Peseta _____
- 🇮🇹 Italian Lira _____

2 Read **How To Use Your Travelers Checks.** Find words or phrases which mean:

a to sign something for the second time
b the person who gives you cash for the check
c the return of lost or stolen money
d the numbers printed on each check

3 Make a conversation:

Student A:	Ask if you can cash a check	Ask to borrow a pen	Ask what the date is	Ask the name of the town	Thank the cashier
Student B:	Agree to cash a check	Lend a pen	Say the date	Say the name	Respond to the thanks

Spelling
You may occasionally see the word, *check*, spelled *cheque*, for example on *American Express Travelers Cheques*. But, the most common spelling in the U.S. is *check*. The U.K. prefer *cheque*.

25 Hotel Lobby

Conversation A
Consuela Rodriguez wants a taxi.

Consuela: Could you call me a cab, please?
Bell Captain: Yes, ma'am. Where are you going?
Consuela: The WorldWide Entertainment Building, downtown.
Bell Captain: Sure, take a seat in the lobby. It'll be five minutes. I'll let you know when it's here.

Conversation B
Jessica Adams has just arrived at the Studios Inn Hotel in Hollywood.

Bell Captain: Welcome to the Studios Inn, ma'am. Are you checking in?
Jessica: Yes.
Bell Captain: Step this way, over to the front desk. I'll look after your bags.
Jessica: Thank you.
Bell Captain: You're welcome. Enjoy your stay.

Conversation C
Keiko Ishida wants her car from the hotel parking lot.

Keiko: Could you get my car, please.
Valet: Sure. What model is it?
Keiko: It's a gray Dodge Dynasty. It's in lot B.
Valet: I'll bring it around right away.

Conversation D
Larry O'Neill is leaving the hotel.

Larry: I'm waiting for the airport courtesy bus.
Bell Captain: Do you have a reservation, sir?
Larry: Yes, I do.
Bell Captain: The bus will be here at 11:00. Take a seat. I'll look after your bags.
Larry: Thank you.

1 **Have similar conversations. Try to replace the key words (in blue) with the words below.**

Conversation A	Conversation B	Conversation C	Conversation D
a L.A. International Airport	**a** Four Seasons Hotel	**a** green / Chevrolet Caprice	**a** 7:30 a.m.
b The train station	**b** Holiday Haven	**b** silver / Lexus	**b** 3:30 p.m.
c City Hall	**c** Regency Hotel	**c** white / Cadillac Seville	**c** 11:30 p.m.
d 3168 Pearson Boulevard	**d** Ritzy	**d** red / Mazda	**d** 10:00 a.m.

26 Fitness Suite

Conversation A

Keiko Ishida: How do I get to the Fitness Suite?
House Keeper: Take this elevator down to the third floor, go across the hall to the Pool Elevator, and that'll take you down to the Fitness Suite.
Keiko Ishida: Thank you.
House Keeper: You're welcome.

Practice giving directions around the hotel.

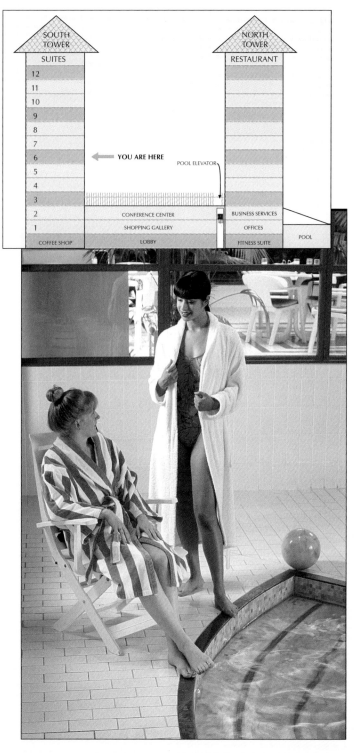

Conversation B
Make similar conversations, using the board from the Fitness Suite.

Attendant: Good morning. Would you sign in, please?
Keiko Ishida: Certainly.
Attendant: Are you a guest?
Keiko Ishida: Yes, I am. I'd like to use the pool.
Attendant: Sure, no problem. Just put your room number after your name. Thanks. I'll get you a towel, Miss Ishida.

FITNESS SUITE
Swimming pool
Jacuzzi
Sauna
Massage Therapist
Weight Machines
Gym *Personal trainer also available*

Operating Hours: 6 a.m. – 10 p.m.

Conversation C
In this dialog, one character introduces herself with both her names. It's polite to reply in the same way.

Woman: Phew! Is it hot enough in here for you?
Keiko Ishida: Yes, it's nice.
Woman: Are you here on business or on vacation?
Keiko Ishida: On business. I'm visiting my company's Los Angeles office.
Woman: Yeah? Is this your first visit to L.A.?
Keiko Ishida: Yes, it is. It's a very interesting place.
Woman: It sure is. Where are you from?
Keiko Ishida: I'm from Kobe, in Japan. Have you heard of it?
Woman: It's near Osaka, isn't it?
Keiko Ishida: That's right. Have you ever been there?
Woman: No, but, I was in Tokyo a couple of years ago. Hey, let me introduce myself. My name's Sue-Ellen Hewitt. I'm from Houston, Texas.
Keiko Ishida: Nice to meet you. I'm Keiko Ishida.

1 Read Conversation C. What facts did you learn about Sue-Ellen Hewitt and Keiko Ishida?

2 In pairs, look at these two business cards.

Dr. D.W.M. Chung M.D.
Welby Hospital
Rm 222
1200 University Ave.
Charlottesville,
Virginia
U.S.A.

Tel: 222 - 0000
Extension: 4321
Pocket Pager: 3421
Emergency: 224 - 0000

ACME FILM COMPANY
17 Haupt Strasse
Schönenberg
Berlin 1000
Germany
Tel: 3331111
Mobile (on location) 7778888
H.R. Schmidt **Production Assistant**

Student A: You are Dr. Chung
Student B: You are H.R. Schmidt

a List as many facts as you can about that person. Name? Job? Place of work? etc.
b Role-play a conversation as that character.

27 Business Services

Consuela Rodriguez is at the Business Services desk in the Studios Inn Hotel.

Consuela: Pardon me, I'd like some help, please.
Clerk: Yes, ma'am. What can I do for you?
Consuela: I want some photocopying done.
Clerk: That's no problem. What do you need?
Consuela: I'd like ten copies of these documents.
Clerk: How many pages are there?
Consuela: Fifteen. I'd like them printed on both sides, collated and stapled.
Clerk: Are you sure you want them stapled? We have some presentation binders if you'd like.
Consuela: May I see them?

Clerk: We have them in gray, white or blue. They're $2.50 each.
Consuela: That's fine. I'll take the blue ones. When will they be ready? I have a meeting at eleven.
Clerk: They'll be ready in half an hour.
Consuela: That's great. Can you charge them to my room account? I'm in 743.
Clerk: Room 743. Just a moment … That's Ms. Rodriguez?
Consuela: Yes, that's right. Thank you. How much will that be?...

1 How much did it cost Consuela?

2 Using the Wordlist (at the back of this book) or a dictionary, find the meaning in your language for the words highlighted.

3 In pairs, have more conversations, and work out the cost.

  a 60 copies / 20 page document
  b 1 color copy / overhead transparency
  c 1 day's cellular phone rental
  d sending a 2 page international fax
  e your own order

Studios Inn Hotel Hollywood Boulevard

BUSINESS SERVICES

Photocopying	.25 ¢ per page
Collating, stapling	15% extra
Presentation binders	$2.50 each
Color copying	$3.00 per page
Overhead transparencies	$6.00 per page
Fax Reception	No charge
Int'l Fax Transmissions	$7.00 for the first page plus $5.00 for each additional one
Computer Rental	$15.00 per hour
Modem use	$10.00 per hour plus telephone line charges
Cellular phone rental	$15.00 per day plus $1.00 per minute

28 Small Talk

Wilbur Meeks is having a business lunch with Marcus Todd, from the Twin Rivers Corporation. This is Wilbur's first meeting with Marcus.

Marcus: Great! Here's the soup. They do an excellent clam chowder here.

Wilbur: So I hear. Now, I wanted to explain more about the contract …

Marcus: I really enjoy seafood. Have you ever been to New Orleans? That's the place for seafood.

Wilbur: No, I haven't. But, you see, my company will be at least 10% cheaper than anyone else and …

Marcus: The weather's been great today. I love the fall. The air feels so crisp.

Wilbur: Did you read our brochure, Mr. Todd? We offer a superb discount for …

Marcus: Wilbur! We can talk business after we eat lunch. Come on, your chowder's getting cold. And just call me Marcus!

Wilbur: Uh huh, sure. Yes … um … Marcus. I just wanted you to look at page ten in the brochure. I have it here.

Marcus: I can see that. It's in your soup!

1 **Find out:**

  a what Marcus suggests Wilbur orders.
  b whether Wilbur has been to New Orleans.
  c where Wilbur's brochure is.

2 **Many people only "talk business" after the meal. What could you talk about during the meal? Look at the list of topics below, and decide whether they would be suitable or not.**

the weather	families	sports
traveling	vacations	work
food and drink	automobiles	music
medical problems	religion	politics
the news	gardening	your country
the environment	money	jokes

3 **Think of a sentence that could introduce each topic. The phrases below will help you.**

Have you ever …?
Are you interested in …?
Did you hear about …?
Do you know …?
How do you feel about …?
Have you been to …?
Do you like …?
What do you think of …?

4 **Make a conversation which introduces all the wrong topics. Then try again with the right ones.**

Ian King, has traveled from Atlanta to Tampa, Florida, on business. His host, Rebecca Larsen, has taken him out to dinner.

Rebecca: Well, Ian, it's a pretty long menu. What would you like?

Ian: This is my first visit to Florida. I'd like to try a local specialty.

Rebecca: Something local? OK … the seafood is always good.

Ian: Sounds fine.

Rebecca: Hey! There's something real local on this menu. You won't find this outside Florida.

Ian: I'll try it! Um … what is it?

Rebecca: Gator tail.

Ian: Pardon?

Rebecca: Gator tail … alligator tail.

Ian: You're kidding.

Rebecca: No, I'm not. It's not real popular. It's just a novelty for the tourists – there's an alligator farm right outside Orlando.

Ian: I don't know …

Rebecca: It tastes just like chicken. You have to try it, Ian. You can tell everyone back home in Britain that you've eaten alligator.

Ian: Well, OK. But only if you have it, too.

Rebecca: Ah. Now, that's a different story! How about some fish? That's a speciality. They have fresh Grouper and Red Snapper. They're both typical of Florida. And of course you just have to try Key Lime Pie for dessert. Now, that's real special …

1 **Read the dialog below.**

> **Student A:** What food is a specialty of <u>France?</u>
> **Student B:** <u>Escargots</u>.
> **Student A:** What's that?
> **Student B:** <u>It's snails.</u>
> **Student A:** Have you ever eaten <u>snails?</u>
> **Student B:** <u>Yes.</u>
> **Student A:** What did <u>they</u> taste like? Did you like <u>them?</u>

Now in pairs, ask and answer similar questions about these other local specialties.

a Japan, Sashimi (raw fish)
b Spain, Gazpacho (chilled vegetable soup)
c Florida, Key Lime Pie (dessert with cream and lime juice)
d New England, Clam Chowder (fish soup with clams)

2 **In the conversation above, find and highlight all the words relating to food.**

3 **Select a menu of local specialties for a visitor to your town or country. Describe the specialties to another person.**

30 On the Phone

Complete Linda's sentences, then listen to the recording and compare.

Jessica Adams: Hello.
Linda Foster: .... Jessica Adams?
Jessica Adams: Speaking.
Linda Foster: .... Linda Foster.
Jessica Adams: What?
Linda Foster: I said, "..................................... ."
Jessica Adams: Who?
Linda Foster: Linda Foster. ....?
Jessica Adams: Not very.................. It's a bad line.
Linda Foster: Linda Foster. That's F for fox-trot, O for ...., S .... , T .... , E .... , R ....
Jessica Adams: Oh, Foster! Linda Foster from Devereux Computers.
Linda Foster: That's right. I'm flying into Chicago from Seattle tomorrow. .... at the Standard Club ....?
Jessica Adams: Yeah, sure, Linda. Ten-thirty at the Standard Club. I'll look forward to seeing you.
Linda Foster: .... Bye.
Jessica Adams: Bye.

1 When Linda Foster could not make Jessica Adams understand her name, she said: "F for fox-trot, O for Oscar," etc. How would you make someone understand these names? Practice in pairs.

a Zimmerman
b Wilson
c Murphy
d Wahlberg
e Kowalski
f Jovanovich
g Quixote
h Danziger
i Potterton
j Fabrizio

2 Linda Foster is flying to Chicago tomorrow. She asked Jessica Adams, "Could you meet me at the Standard Club at 10:30?" Make similar requests for these places and times.

a the corner of Clark and Adams – 2:45
b Hartsfield Airport – 4:00
c the Health Club – 11:15
d the Union Building – 3:30
e Willowby's Restaurant – 1:00

3 What features does this phone have? Explain them.

☎	TELEPHONE FEATURES	
dial 9	for outside call
**1	re-dial
# * 9 + xtn no.	transfer
# 3 + xtn nos.	conference call
#	do not disturb
**4	hold

31 Telephone Facilities

Operator: Operator.
Michael Robertson: May I have the number for directory assistance?
Operator: Is this for long distance assistance?
Michael Robertson: Yes.
Operator: You dial 1, then the area code, then 5 - 5 - 5, 1 - 2 - 1 - 2.
Michael Robertson: Sure, OK. But, what is the area code for Hollywood?
Operator: It's 2 - 1 - 3.
Michael Robertson: Thank you.

Hollywood Operator: Hello. Directory Assistance. What's the name and address that you require?
Michael Robertson: Studios Inn Hotel, Hollywood Boulevard.
Operator: Just one moment, please.
Recorded message: The number is area code 2 - 1 - 3, 1 - 3 - 1, 6 - 8 - 5 - 3.

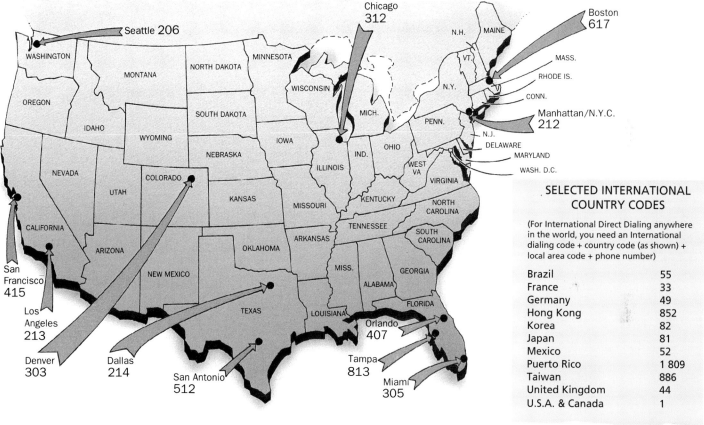

SELECTED INTERNATIONAL COUNTRY CODES

(For International Direct Dialing anywhere in the world, you need an International dialing code + country code (as shown) + local area code + phone number)

Brazil	55
France	33
Germany	49
Hong Kong	852
Korea	82
Japan	81
Mexico	52
Puerto Rico	1 809
Taiwan	886
United Kingdom	44
U.S.A. & Canada	1

1 In pairs, look at the key language (in blue). Make similar conversations using these names and addresses:

Superior Travel, 2456 Sandlake Road, Orlando, Florida

Wilbur Meeks, 17862 Simpson Drive, Seattle, Washington

Jessica Adams, Apt. 45, The Illinois Tower, Chicago

Sandra Buchman, 1530A Elm St. New York City

2 When Michael Robertson called the Studios Inn Hotel, he heard a recorded message. The message told him that he could use a touch-tone phone to contact various numbers directly. Listen to the recording. What were the touch-tone numbers for these locations?

Location	Number
Hotel Reservations	
Hotel Management	
Guest Rooms	
Guest Services	
Conference Center	
Business Services	

3 Look at the codes. You're in Hollywood. What numbers do you need when dialing direct to:

Boston / Denver / Puerto Rico / San Antonio / Japan / France / Tampa / Mexico.

4 Discuss:

- Where have you called long distance?
- Do you dial direct or go through the operator?
- When calling long distance, have you ever called the wrong number? Where to? What happened?

32 Duty-Free

Natalie Trudeau has stopped over at Heathrow Airport in Britain on her way from Paris to Los Angeles.

Demonstrator: Are you buying whisky today, madam?

Natalie: I'm not sure. I'm just looking.

Demonstrator: We have a special offer on liters of Glenfiddich malt whisky. It's very good value.

Natalie: How much whisky am I allowed to take into the United States?

Demonstrator: There's a chart over there. Would you like to try a sample?

Natalie: No, thank you. Is a liter more than a quart?

Demonstrator: No, it's less than a quart. We also have quarts of Glenfiddich.

Natalie: Well, I'll think about it. Thank you.

Cashier: That's £29.85.

Natalie: Can I pay in dollars?

Cashier: Yes, of course. That'll be $53.75.

Natalie: Oh, dear. I only have 50 dollars, and I'm right out of pounds, too.

Cashier: You can pay by credit card.

Natalie: Oh, wait a second. I have some French Francs.

Cashier: That's fine, but I'll have to give you the change in English money.

Natalie: No problem.

Cashier: OK. Can I see your boarding pass, please?

Duty-Free Allowance Chart — London Heathrow

Destination		Cigarettes	Cigars	Tobacco	Wine	Spirits	Perfume
European Community		200	or 50	or 250 gm	2 litres	1 litre	50 grams
Japan	visitors	400	or 100	or 500 gm	3 bottles	or 3 bottles	2 oz
	residents	200	or 50	or 250 gm	3 bottles	or 3 bottles	2 oz
Saudi Arabia		600	or 100	or 500 gm	Strictly prohibited		for personal use
USA	visitors-gifts	Nil	100*	one carton	Nil	Nil	no limit
	visitors-personal use	200	or 50	or 3 pounds	1 US quart	or 1 US quart	no limit
	residents	200	or 100	no limit*	1 litre	or 1 litre	no limit*

* cost deducted from personal allowance

① In pairs, look at the Duty-Free Allowance Chart. Make conversations using this pattern:

How much whisky am I allowed to take into *France?*
How many cigars am I allowed to take into *Japan*?

② Are these statements true [✓] or false [✗] ?

a ☐ You're not allowed to take any alcohol to Saudi Arabia.

b ☐ You are allowed to take 30 bottles of wine to Japan.

c ☐ You are not allowed take more than 1 liter of spirits to the European Community.

d ☐ You can only take 50 cigarettes into Saudi Arabia.

e ☐ You can pay in foreign currencies at most international airports.

f ☐ A quart is smaller than a liter.

g ☐ Visitors are allowed to take spirits into the U.S.A. only for personal use.

h ☐ Glenfiddich is a type of wine.

Spelling

Whiskey/whisky : On the label you may notice – Whiskey from Ireland and the U.S.A. is spelled with an "e". Whisky from Scotland, Canada and Japan is always spelled without an "e".

③ Discuss:

• Make a list of items you can buy at duty-free stores. Compare it with your partner.

• Do you think duty-free stores are cheaper?

• Why do you think there are limits on the amount of duty-free goods you can buy?

Conversation A

Wilbur Meeks had to go to Boston on business. He's now waiting for his baggage at the baggage claim.

Woman: I hate waiting for baggage, don't you?
Wilbur: Oh, yes. Mine always seems to be the last.
Woman: I'm always so nervous. Last year they lost my suitcase. Have they ever lost yours?
Wilbur: Mine? No.
Woman: Ah! There's my bag now. Right, I've got it. Bye.

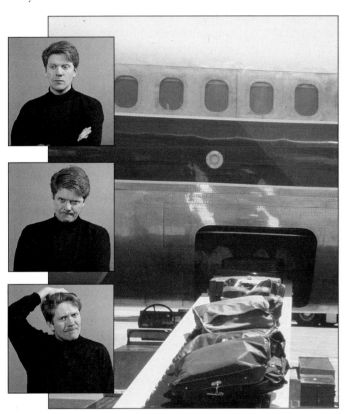

Conversation B

Wilbur: Ah, excuse me. My bag hasn't arrived yet.
Airline Representative: Which flight?
Wilbur: Um, Redwood Airlines from Seattle.
Airline Representative: RRA 438?
Wilbur: Pardon me?
Airline Representative: The flight number. RRA 438?
Wilbur: Yes. Everyone else's bags came off the baggage claim, and now it's stopped. But mine never arrived.
Airline Representative: Uh huh. Did it have your name and address on it?
Wilbur: It had my name, address, zip code and telephone number.
Airline Representative: We'll try to find it for you, sir. Can you fill out this form? Description of bag, flight number, value of contents etc.
Wilbur: Oh. Yes.
Airline Representative: Do you have an itemized list of the contents?
Wilbur: No. Why?
Airline Representative: Your insurance company might ask for an itemized list. You'd better write one.
Wilbur: OK.
Airline Representative: And don't worry. Ninety percent of lost bags turn up someplace.
Wilbur: I hope so.
Airline Representative: If it doesn't turn up within twelve hours your insurance will pay for the things you need right now - a clean shirt, socks, underwear, that kind of thing.

---

1 Write an itemized list of the things you would pack for a business trip to either a hot climate or a cold one. Interview another person and find out what they would take.

2 In Conversations A and B, find and highlight the past tense of these verbs.

- [ ] come
- [ ] lose
- [ ] arrive
- [ ] stop

3 Listen to the recording of Conversation C. Where did Wilbur's suitcase go? Check the boxes.

- [ ] Bangkok
- [ ] Hong Kong
- [ ] Baltimore
- [ ] Boston
- [ ] Las Vegas
- [ ] Rome
- [ ] Bombay
- [ ] Beijing
- [ ] New York
- [ ] Los Angeles
- [ ] Seattle
- [ ] Bologna

4 Using the Wordlist (at the back of this book) or a dictionary, find the meaning, in your language, for the words highlighted.

5 Discuss:

- Has an airline ever lost your baggage?
- Was it lost forever or was it found?
- Do you take out travel insurance when you fly?
- Have you ever made a travel insurance claim?

34 Airport Arrivals

Try to complete Tadashi's answers to the Immigration Inspector's questions. Then listen to the recording and compare your answers.

Immigration Inspector: Good morning. Where have you come from?
Tadashi Nakamura: ....
....
....

Immigration Inspector: Fine. May I see your passport?
Tadashi Nakamura: ....
....

Immigration Inspector: What's the nature of your visit?
Tadashi Nakamura: ....
....
....

Immigration Inspector: And how long are you staying in the United States?
Tadashi Nakamura: ....
....
....

Immigration Inspector: Fine. Here's your passport back.
Tadashi Nakamura: ....
....

Immigration Inspector: Welcome to the United States. Enjoy your stay.

Welcome to the United States

Admission Number:
234199692 01

I-94 Arrival/Departure Record

This form must be completed by all persons except U.S. citizens, returning resident aliens, aliens with immigration visas and Canadian citizens visiting, or in transit.

Type or print legibly with a pen in ALL CAPITAL LETTERS. Use English. Do not write on the back of this form.

This form is in two parts. Please complete both the Arrival Record (Items 1 through 13) and the Departure Record (Items 14 through 17.)

When all items are completed, present this form to the U.S. Immigration and Naturalization Service Inspector.

Item 7 - If you are entering the United States by land enter LAND in this space. If you are entering the United States by sea, write SEA, in this space.

Admission Number
234196692 01   I-94 Arrival Record

1. Family name NAKAMURA
2. First (Given) name TADASHI
3. Birth date (Day / Mo / Yr) 020771
4. Country of citizenship JAPAN
5. Sex (Male or female) MALE
6. Passport number AB12345
7. Airline & Flight Number AN 452
8. Country where you live JAPAN
9. City where you boarded TOKYO
10. City where visa was issued TOKYO
11. Date issued (Day / Mo / Yr) 14 21 95
12. Address while you are in the United States (number and street) 1313 HOLLYWOOD BLVD.
13. City and State HOLLYWOOD CALIFORNIA

Departure Number
234196692 01   I-94 Departure Record

14. Family name
15. First (Given) name
16. Birth date (Day / Mo / Yr)
17. Country of Citizenship

Staple Here

I-94 FORM

As a foreign national (exce Canadian citizens and U.S. are required to fill out an I- form. This form will be give you during the flight.

- Please provide your personal d and travel-related information.
- Please fill out only the front side do not use the reverse side.
- This form must be kept in your passport until you leave the U.S.A
- One form is required for every member of the family.
- Please complete the I-94 form legib in English and in capital letters.

me to the United States

...Arrival/Departure Record
...d by all persons except U.S. citizens, ...immigration visas and Canadian citizer
...pen in ALL CAPITAL LETTERS. U this form.
...ease complete both the Arrival Recor ... Departure Record (Items 14 throug ...d, present this form to the U.S. Imm ...ctor.
...he United States by land enter LAN ... United States by sea, write SEA, i

Admission Number
234196692 02   I-94 Arrival Record

1. Family name
2. First (Given) name
3. Bir
4. Country of citizenship
5. Sex
6. Passport number
7. Airline
8. Country where you live
9. City wh
10. City where visa was issued
11. Date issued (Day / Mo / Yr)
12. Address while you are in the United States (number and street)
13. City and State

Departure Number
234196692 02   I-94 Departure Record

14. Family name
15. First (Given) name
16. Birth date (Day / Mo / Yr)
17. Country of Citizenship

1 Look at this part of the conversation.

Immigration Inspector: How long are you staying in the United States?
Tadashi Nakamura: About three weeks.

In pairs, ask and answer questions like this, using these words:

a at the Hilton / three days
b in Paris / a week
c in Seoul / twenty-four hours
d at the Park Towers / five days
e in London / two weeks

2 Interview another student and complete the I-94 form with their details.

3 With a partner, role-play a conversation with an Immigration Inspector.

4 What experiences have you had going through Passport or Immigration check points?

35 Customs

Customs Officer: Excuse me. Do you have anything to declare?

Tadashi Nakamura: No, nothing. Just the normal allowance.

Customs Officer: Have you read the customs form, sir?

Tadashi Nakamura: Yes, I have.

Customs Officer: OK then, could you open up your suitcase for me, please?

Tadashi Nakamura: Sure.

Customs Officer: That's fine, thank you. You can proceed.

Tadashi Nakamura: Thanks.

Customs Officer: Enjoy your stay in the United States.

Plants

Liquor-filled candy

Meats

Fruits/Vegetables

Ivory

CAUTION: Some Prohibited Items

CUSTOMS FORM

Before arriving in the U.S., each traveler (or head of family) is required to fill out a Customs Declaration Form.

- Please complete the form in English and in capital letters.
- Most of the questions on the Customs Declaration Form can be answered by writing "Yes" or "No".
- Please remember to sign your name at the bottom of the reverse side.
- This form will be distributed during the flight.

WELCOME TO THE UNITED STATES
CUSTOMS DECLARATION

Each arriving traveler or head of family must provide the following information (only **ONE** declaration per family is required)

1. Name: ....
   Last   first   middle

2. Date of Birth: .... 3. Airline/Flight ....

4. Number of family members traveling with you ....

5. U.S. Address: ....
   City: .... State: ....

6. I am a U.S. Citizen   Tick boxes   YES ☐ NO ☐
   If No. Country: ....

7. I reside permanently in the U.S.   Tick boxes   YES ☐ NO ☐
   If No. Expected length of stay: ....

8. The purpose of my trip is or was   Tick box   BUSINESS ☐   PLEASURE ☐

9. I am/we are bringing fruits, plants, meats, food, soil, birds, snails, other live animals, farm products, or I/we have been on a farm or ranch outside the U.S.   YES ☐ NO ☐

10. I am/we are carrying currency or monetary instruments over $10,000 U.S. or foreign equivalent.   YES ☐ NO ☐

11. The total value of goods I/we purchased or acquired abroad and am/are bringing to the U.S. is (see instruction under Merchandise on reverse side): $.........................
    U.S. Dollars

MOST MAJOR CREDIT CARDS ACCEPTED.
SIGN ON REVERSE SIDE AFTER YOU HAVE READ THIS WARNING.
(Don't write below this line)

Inspectors Name	Stamp area
Badge No.	

PLEASE TURN OVER

---

❶ Complete the sentences below. Then listen to the recording and compare.

Customs Officer: Excuse me. Do you have ....
.... ?

Natalie Trudeau: Well, I ....

Customs Officer: How .... whiskey ....
.... ?

Natalie Trudeau: ....
....

Customs Officer: That's OK. Do ....…
anything else?

Natalie Trudeau: .... perfume.

Customs Officer: There .... restrictions on perfume for personal use. Is that all?

Natalie Trudeau: ....

Customs Officer: That's OK. You can go through.

❷ Look at the Customs Declaration. Imagine you are entering the United States and complete this form. Interview another student and find out what's on their form.

❸ Discuss:

- Is it important to have customs at international borders. Why?/Why not?
- What kind of items do people try to smuggle?
- Could more be done to stop smugglers?

36 Asking for Directions

① **Look at the map. Find abbreviations for:**

Boulevard   Avenue
Street

② **Then find:**
a somewhere you can take a train from
b a motion picture studio
c somewhere you can watch a baseball game
d a famous church
e somewhere you can find Asian restaurants

③ **Find the Hollywood High School. This is your starting point. Listen to Conversations A, B, and C, and follow the directions.**

④ **Choose a location and give directions to another person. They should follow the route on the map. Use the directions in the boxes to help.**

Go	left.
Turn	right.
Take a	

Go	straight ahead.
	across (15th Street).
	down / up (15th Street).
	past (the...).
	north / south / east / west.
	through the intersection of ... and ...

Take the	(first) exit on your (right).
	exit 15A.
	second turn on your (right).

You'll see it.
You can't miss it.

37 Time Zones

Mr. Devereux: Hello? This is Max Devereux.

Wilbur Meeks: Good morning, Mr. Devereux. How are you today?

Mr. Devereux: What the ... Who is this?

Wilbur Meeks: It's me Mr. Devereux. Wilbur Meeks, calling from the Boston office. I'm sorry to call you at home, sir, but I ...

Mr. Devereux: Wilbur? Do you know what time it is?

Wilbur Meeks: Yes, sir. It's eight a.m.

Mr. Devereux: But do you know what time it is here in Seattle?

Wilbur Meeks: Yes, sir. It's eleven a.m. Pacific Time.

Mr. Devereux: Wilbur! Pacific Time is three hours *behind* Eastern Standard Time, not three hours ahead!

Wilbur Meeks: Oh! You mean ...

Mr Devereux: I mean it's five o'clock in the morning! This had better be very important, Wilbur. Wilbur? Are you there? Huh. He hung up on me!

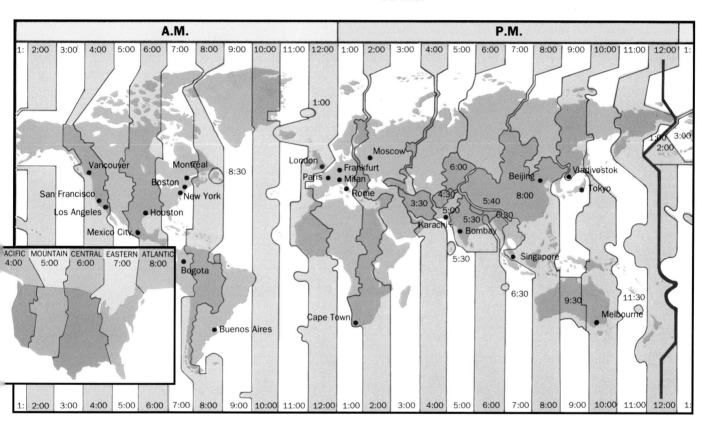

1 **Study the map and answer these questions.**

  a When it's 5 p.m. in Boston, what is the time in:

Los Angeles	Tokyo
Paris	Moscow
London	Mexico City

  b When it's 3 a.m. in Bombay, what time is it in:

Cape Town	Rome
Melbourne	Bogota
Beijing	Buenos Aires

2 **Study the map. Choose eight cities and make sentences like this:**

When it's 7 p.m. in Paris, it's 12 noon in Mexico City.
When it's 3 p.m. in Milan, it's midnight in Vladivostok.
When it's 6 p.m. in New York, it's 10 a.m. the next day in Tokyo.

3 **Find out:**

  a How many hours is Montreal ahead of Vancouver?
  b How many hours is Karachi behind Singapore?

4 **Ask another student more questions like those in question 3.**

5 **Decide on two cities and two times, and practice a telephone conversation.**

38 A Job Interview

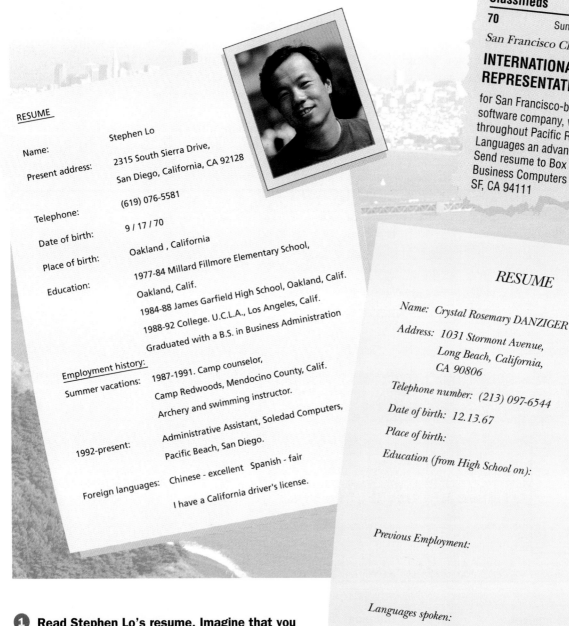

RESUME

Name: Stephen Lo

Present address: 2315 South Sierra Drive,
                     San Diego, California, CA 92128

Telephone: (619) 076-5581

Date of birth: 9 / 17 / 70

Place of birth: Oakland , California

Education: 1977-84 Millard Fillmore Elementary School,
                     Oakland, Calif.
                     1984-88 James Garfield High School, Oakland, Calif.
                     1988-92 College. U.C.L.A., Los Angeles, Calif.
                     Graduated with a B.S. in Business Administration

Employment history:
Summer vacations: 1987-1991. Camp counselor,
                     Camp Redwoods, Mendocino County, Calif.
                     Archery and swimming instructor.

1992-present: Administrative Assistant, Soledad Computers,
                     Pacific Beach, San Diego.

Foreign languages: Chinese - excellent   Spanish - fair

                     I have a California driver's license.

RESUME

Name: Crystal Rosemary DANZIGER

Address: 1031 Stormont Avenue,
Long Beach, California,
CA 90806

Telephone number: (213) 097-6544

Date of birth: 12.13.67

Place of birth:

Education (from High School on):

Previous Employment:

Languages spoken:

Driver's license:

1 Read Stephen Lo's resume. Imagine that you are interviewing Stephen for the job. What questions would you ask him?

2 Next listen to the recording of Stephen Lo's interview (Conversation A) and compare your questions with the recorded interview.

3 Listen to the recorded interview with Crystal Danziger (Conversation B). How much of her resume can you complete?

4 Who would you give the job to? Why?

5 Write your own resume. Interview another student and find out what is written on their resume.

39 An Application Form

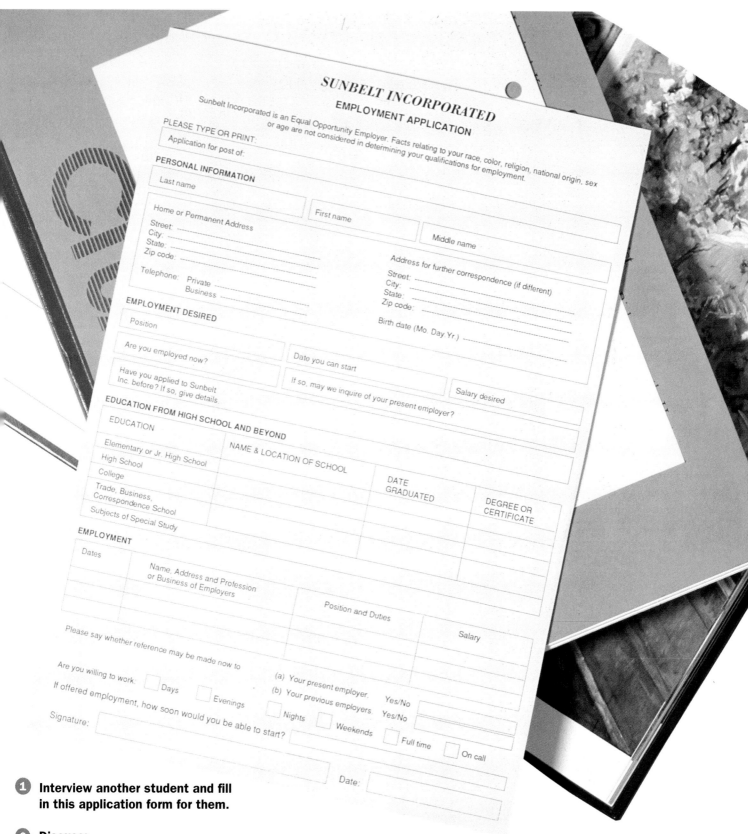

SUNBELT INCORPORATED
EMPLOYMENT APPLICATION

Sunbelt Incorporated is an Equal Opportunity Employer. Facts relating to your race, color, religion, national origin, sex or age are not considered in determining your qualifications for employment.

PLEASE TYPE OR PRINT.
Application for post of:

PERSONAL INFORMATION

Last name

First name

Home or Permanent Address
Street:
City:
State:
Zip code:

Middle name

Address for further correspondence (if different)
Street:
City:
State:
Zip code:

Telephone: Private
Business

EMPLOYMENT DESIRED

Position

Birth date (Mo. Day.Yr.)

Are you employed now?

Date you can start

Have you applied to Sunbelt Inc. before? If so, give details.

If so, may we inquire of your present employer?

Salary desired

EDUCATION FROM HIGH SCHOOL AND BEYOND

EDUCATION	NAME & LOCATION OF SCHOOL	DATE GRADUATED	DEGREE OR CERTIFICATE
Elementary or Jr. High School			
High School			
College			
Trade, Business, Correspondence School			
Subjects of Special Study			

EMPLOYMENT

Dates	Name, Address and Profession or Business of Employers	Position and Duties	Salary

Please say whether reference may be made now to

Are you willing to work: ☐ Days   ☐ Evenings   ☐ Nights   ☐ Weekends   ☐ Full time   ☐ On call

(a) Your present employer.   Yes/No
(b) Your previous employers.   Yes/No

If offered employment, how soon would you be able to start?

Signature:

Date:

1 Interview another student and fill in this application form for them.

2 Discuss:
- If you were interviewing someone for a job at your company, what qualities or experience would you look for?
- If you were being interviewed, what qualities would you look for in your employer?

40 Breakfast in America

Ian King is at the Sheraton Century Center in Atlanta. Try to complete the conversation, then listen to the recording and compare.

Waitress: Hi! .... ? Are you ready to order?

Ian King: Yes, I am, thank you. .... the Farmer's Breakfast.

Waitress: .... your eggs – sunnyside-up, over-easy, or ...

Ian King: Sunnyside-up?

Waitress: Oh, I see. You're British! Well, that's when the egg's not flipped over. You can also have your eggs poached or scrambled.

Ian King: Uh, ... sunnyside-up.

Waitress: .... link sausage, bacon, or country ham?

Ian King: .... please. Instead of the grits .... pancakes?

Waitress: Sorry, sir. I'm afraid the pancakes .... be a side order.

Ian King: All right, then. .... of pancakes.

Waitress: Anything to drink?

Ian King: .... A coffee, please, and freshly-squeezed orange juice.

Waitress: Cream and sugar are .... I'll bring your coffee .... right away.

Ian King: .... a glass of water?

Waitress: Sure. Coming right up.

1
a In which ways can Ian King have his eggs cooked?
b What does sunnyside-up mean?
c What's a side order?
d What did Ian King ask for as a side order?
e What's included in a Farmer's Breakfast?

2 **What do people eat for breakfast in your country and other countries you've been to? How is it different from American breakfasts?**

3 **Ask your partner what they would like for breakfast tomorrow and fill in the card.**

American Breakfasts
American breakfasts are usually very large, but you can get a light continental breakfast in your room, or you can choose from a buffet, or off the menu.

PLEASE HANG ROOM SERVICE BREAKFAST ORDER OUTSIDE DOOR BEFORE 2:00 A.M.

ROOM SERVICE BREAKFAST

Indicate number of breakfasts, time required and check each item required.

No. of breakfasts required: ☐   Room no. ☐   Date: ☐

☐ 6–6:30   ☐ 6:30–7   ☐ 7–7:30   ☐ 7:30–8
☐ 8–8:30   ☐ 8:30–9   ☐ 9–9:30   ☐ 9:30–10
☐ 10–10:30   ☐ Other time (available 24 hours)

Juice: ☐ Orange   ☐ Grapefruit   ☐ Tomato
Yoghurt: ☐ Natural   ☐ Blueberry   ☐ Fruit flavored Low Fat
Cereals: ☐ Cornflakes   ☐ Branflakes   ☐ Granola
☐ Cheerios   ☐ Oatmeal
Drinks: ☐ Coffee   ☐ Decaff. coffee   ☐ Tea ☐ Milk
Breads: ☐ Muffins   ☐ Croissants   ☐ Danish
☐ Wholewheat Rolls ☐ Toast
Selection of jams/jellies, honey, butter, low-fat spread

Guest signature

15% Service Charge added to all Room Service orders. Sales tax will be adde

41 Conversations

Conversation A
The best way to start a conversation is to ask questions.
Keiko Ishida has just been introduced to Natalie Trudeau from WorldWide Entertainment.

Keiko: … WorldWide Entertainment? Do you know Paul Steinway from your New York office?
Natalie: Well, I don't know him personally, but I've spoken to him on the phone. I work in our Paris office.
Keiko: I met Paul last year.
Natalie: Oh, really, where?
Keiko: At the film festival in Osaka. He was with a bearded man - I can't remember his name.
Natalie: A tall guy with a beard, and glasses?
Keiko: That's right.
Natalie: Oh! That was Ryan Thomas. He works here in L.A.

Conversation B

If you've met someone's family, it's polite to ask about them.
Consuela Rodriguez has just arrived at WorldWide Entertainment's Los Angeles office.

Ryan Thomas: Consuela! Come in. It's great to see you again.
Consuela: It's good to see you, too. How's Marguerite?
Ryan Thomas: She's fine.
Consuela: And how are the kids?
Ryan Thomas: They're fine. Laura's just started First Grade.
Consuela: Really? How does she like it?
Ryan Thomas: She loves it … so far. How's Enrique?
Consuela: Working too hard … as usual! He sends his regards.
Ryan Thomas: Thank you. Marguerite says that while you're here, you must come over and visit us.
Consuela: I'd love to.
Ryan Thomas: Great. Is tomorrow evening OK?
Consuela: That's fine.

1 **Listen to Conversation A and answer these questions:**
a Which office does Paul Steinway work in?
b Where does Natalie work?
c What does Ryan Thomas look like?
d Where did Keiko meet Ryan and Paul?

2 **In Conversation B highlight:**
a a greeting
b a question about the family
c an invitation
d an acceptance

3 **Discuss. In your country, do you …**
• exchange business cards?
• ask about business acquaintances' families?
• ask about their colleagues?
• invite business contacts to your home?

Why?/Why not?

42 Describing People

Rebecca Johnson

Zachary Johnson

Jacob Fielding

Jennifer Michaels

Steve Michaels

Brittany Barnes-Fielding

1 **Ask and answer questions like this about the characters.**

Which one is Jacob Fielding?
He's the man with a beard.

Who's the man with a beard?
That's Jacob Fielding.

2 **Look at the diagram below. Who's sitting where? Write their initials in the boxes on the table.**

a The man with glasses is sitting across from the man with dark hair.

b The woman with short, dark, curly hair can see herself in the mirror, and is sitting between the man with the beard, and the man with dark hair.

c The man with the beard is sitting on the left of the woman with glasses.

d The woman with glasses is sitting across from the woman with short, dark, curly hair.

e The woman with long blonde hair is sitting between the man with the dark hair, and the man with the glasses.

MIRROR

3 **Look at the language below and ask questions.**

Your partner answers:
Yes, he/she is – Yes, he/she has
No, he/she isn't – No, he/she doesn't have

Is Was	Rebecca Johnson Zachary Johnson Jacob Fielding Jennifer Michaels	bald? tall? blonde? slim? short? large? attractive? handsome? bearded? dark-haired?

Does Did	Rebecca Johnson Zachary Johnson Jennifer Michaels Jacob Fielding	have	dark hair? a beard? brown eyes? a mustache? long hair? blonde hair?

43 The Office Party

Scott and Ashley Moreton are at Scott's office party.

Ashley: Scott, who's that man **who's** talking so loudly?

Scott: Which one? Everybody's talking loudly.

Ashley: The bald man with the mustache.

Scott: Oh, him! That's Harrison. He's the company president.

Ashley: And that woman **who's** standing next to him. Is she his wife?

Scott: The one with the gray hair? Why do you think she's his wife?

Ashley: She's the only one **who** isn't laughing at his jokes!

Scott: But everyone else has to! Same again, honey?

Ashley: No, thanks. I'll just have a mineral water.

Man: Hello, I haven't seen you before.

Ashley: That's because I don't work here. My husband does.

Man: Oh, what's his name?

Ashley: Scott. Scott Moreton. Do you know him?

Man: No. I don't work here either - my girlfriend does. I suppose she knows him.

Ashley: Where is she?

Man: She's over there. That attractive, blonde girl **who**'s talking to that funny-looking man with the beard and glasses. I wonder who he is?

Ashley: That "funny-looking man" is my husband!

1
 a What is the name of the company president?
 b What does he look like?
 c Why isn't his wife laughing?
 d What does Ashley have to drink?

2 **Look at the language in the box and make more sentences using these words.**

That	tall	man	who	's talking.
She's the	blonde	woman	that	was over there.
He's the	young	person		owns the company.
I don't know the	short	guy		spoke to you.

3 **Connect these sentences using *who*.**
 a He's the very good-looking guy. He's telling them about computers.
 b She's the small gray-haired woman. She works for Devereux Computers.
 c She's the person. She's just bought a drink.
 d They're the ones. They work for C.B.W.
 e That's the person. She works in the Design Department.

44 A Better Computer

Jessica: Michael! Hi, come in. What can I do for you?

Michael: There are a couple of things, Jessica. First I wanted to thank you for all your help.

Jessica: You're very welcome, Michael.

Michael: Secondly, I wanted to ask you about your computer system. It really is excellent. It's much better than the one we use at C.B.W. It's faster, and I think it's much easier to operate.

Jessica: We've been very happy with it. It's probably less expensive, too.

Michael: All the software comes from Devereux Computers, doesn't it?

Jessica: Yes. They're a Seattle company. They're the best in their field.

Michael: Yes, I know, I asked them for some information. It seems they don't have a Canadian distributor anymore.

Jessica: That surprises me. I know Max Devereux well, and Seattle's close to the Canadian border.

Michael: Right. Well, it seems that their Canadian distributor went out of business recently.

Jessica: Is that so?

Michael: Yes, well, I'd like to meet this Mr. Devereux. Maybe we can make a deal.

Jessica: Are you going to the International Convention of Civil Engineers, in L.A.?

Michael: Yes.

Jessica: Well, Devereux Computers will have an exhibit there. I can introduce you to Max.

Michael: Are you sure it's no trouble?

Jessica: No, not at all. Max is one of my oldest friends. Maybe I can do you both a favor!

1 Look at the sentences in the box, and practice saying them.

The computer system is …	The system is …
…faster.	…the best.
…better.	…the fastest.
…newer.	…the cheapest.
…easier to operate.	…the most expensive.
…more expensive.	…the least expensive.
…less expensive.	…the most/least sophisticated.
…more/less sophisticated.	
…more/less modern.	

2 In groups. Use the sentences from the box, and compare any of the items listed below.

a computers (Macintosh, Amiga & IBM)

b cars (Cadillac, Toyota Corolla, Mazda RX-7)

c hotels (5 star, 3 star, 2 star)

d travel (by road, train, air)

3 Find out about another person's computer. Is it better, or faster, or more expensive than yours? What can it do?

45 Presentations

Wilbur Meeks has to give a presentation to Devereux Computers marketing department, at their annual sales conference in Seattle.

Wilbur needs to display information about sales in the West Coast area. He has figures for five states: California, Oregon, Washington, Nevada and Arizona. Look at the different ways this information is displayed. Which should Wilbur use? Why?

Table

Sales Figures: West Coast Area

California	$17,500,000
Oregon	$ 3,500,000
Washington	$7,000,000
Nevada	$1,500,000
Arizona	$500,000

Bar Graph

Pie Chart

Map

1 **How should he present this information?**

☐ photocopied handouts

☐ overhead projector

☐ computer graphics

2 **Should he use color or monochrome?**

3 **What equipment will he need for a computer graphics presentation?**

☐ computer
☐ video projector
☐ overhead projector
☐ video screen
☐ keyboard
☐ presentation software

4 **Is it worth using computer graphics?**

5 **Look at the state populations. Which state has the highest sales in proportion to its population?**

State Populations (1990 U.S. Census)

California	29,839,250
Oregon	2,853,733
Washington	4,887,941
Nevada	1,206,152
Arizona	3,677,985

All Devereux products are available in MS-DOS and Macintosh versions

DEV COMPLETE OFFICE

("The best value on the market" – Personally Computing)
New integrated software package. Ideal for small business user. Includes word processor, spreadsheet, database and graphics program. All that most small businesses require.
$1695 Product code: 70084

DEV DRAW Version 6.15

("Fast, powerful and user-friendly" – Mac Pac Magazine)
Latest version of our popular graphics program which has both PAINT and DRAW capabilities.
Compatible with MS Windows/Mac System 7.
$425 Product code: 60091

DEV MEANS BUSINESS 1.0

("Perhaps the easiest database available" – Compute!)
Includes speadsheets, database, charting capability.
$495 Product code: 50089

DEV WRITE TWO

("The word processor with every feature you will ever need "– MS-DOS Weekly)
Medium-priced word processing package with thesaurus, grammar checker and 100,000-word spelling checker. Includes voice annotation software and full macro facility.
$630 Product code: 50081

DEV DTP 2.0

("Highly professional DTP software at a price even beginners can afford" – Mac Pac Magazine)
Desktop publishing software which can import files from most popular word processing and graphics programs.
$799 Product code: 50036

DEV PRESENTS ...

("The most exciting presentations software package this year" – Orlando News)
The newest presentation package on the market. Sample disk on request. See it, use it. You'll buy it!
$399 Product code: 40071

NOW TURN TO:

⇨ Games (page 21)	
⇨ Disk drives (page 22)	
⇨ Scanners (page 23)	
⇨ CD- ROM (page 24)	

Quantity discount on orders over 20 units.
Quoted prices are for single-users.
Please inquire for multiple-user prices.

---

1 Read the page from Devereux Computers' latest brochure.

Then listen to the recording of Wilbur Meeks describing three of the packages. Which one is he describing?

1st description	
2nd description	
3rd description	

2 Make out an order for three of the programs.

Quantity	Product Code	Price Per Package	MS-DOS or Macintosh	Total Cost ($) (Quantity x Price)

3 Everyone wants something different from their computer. In groups, discuss the ideal integrated software system. What will it do? How much will it cost? Write a product description.

47 A Market Survey

SURVEY

DEVEREUX COMPUTERS

The Wilson Building, Chester Street, Seattle, WA 60014

We would appreciate it if you would take the time to fill out this computer survey. The results will be very helpful in determining the best computer software and hardware for your business and/or leisure computer needs. Please check the appropriate box.

1 You are: female ☐ male ☐ under 25 ☐ 26-40 ☐ 41-60 ☐ over 60 ☐

2 Do you use a computer at:
(Please check all that apply.)
your place of work? ☐
your home for work? ☐
your home for personal use? ☐ other _____ ? ☐

3 Which types of software do you most use?
(Please check all that apply.)
spreadsheet ☐ inventory database ☐ games ☐
word processing ☐ design/graphics ☐ other _____ ☐

4 Which types of hardware do you most use?
(Please check all that apply)
printer ☐ large storage capacity ☐ mouse ☐ optical drive ☐
keyboard ☐ modem ☐ CD-Rom drive ☐ scanner ☐

5 Do you own a computer? Yes ☐ No ☐
If so, what type of computer do you have? _____

6 Do you own a printer? Yes ☐ No ☐
If so, what type of printer (LaserWriter, Ink-Jet, etc.) do you have? _____

7 Please fill in your name and address if you are interested in receiving information about computers and computer software currently available.

Mr./Ms./Dr. _____

Address _____

Zip code _____ Telephone _____

① **Fill out this survey, then compare in groups.**

② **Discuss why Devereux Computers wants this information and how they might use it.**

③ **You work for Best Computers which is a chain of computer stores in Canada. Write a letter to Devereux Computers, asking where you can get Devereux products in Canada.**

BEST COMPUTERS

5000 Dufferin Street Unit K Toronto, Ontario G4T 3S2

Devereux Computers
The Wilson Building
Chester Street
Seattle WA 600 14

(date)

④ **Write a reply from Devereux Computers. Inform Best Computers that you have no distributor in Canada. Offer to supply them from your Head Office in Seattle.**

48 Talking About Vacations

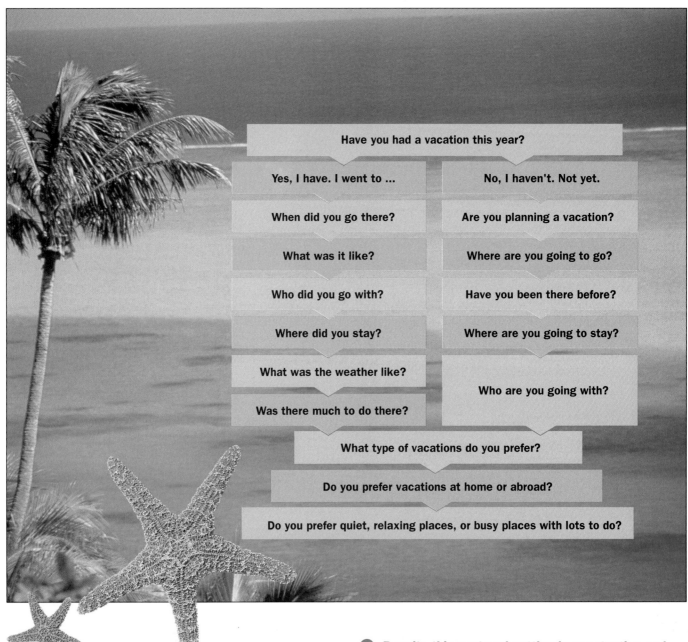

Have you had a vacation this year?

| Yes, I have. I went to ... | No, I haven't. Not yet. |

| When did you go there? | Are you planning a vacation? |

| What was it like? | Where are you going to go? |

| Who did you go with? | Have you been there before? |

| Where did you stay? | Where are you going to stay? |

| What was the weather like? | Who are you going with? |

Was there much to do there?

What type of vacations do you prefer?

Do you prefer vacations at home or abroad?

Do you prefer quiet, relaxing places, or busy places with lots to do?

After you have talked about the weather, food, and the town you are visiting, vacations are one of the most popular topics of conversation.

1. Use the ideas in the chart above and interview two other students about their vacations.

2. What kind of vacation would be best for these people. Why?

   a a business executive wanting to relax
   b an active family
   c a honeymoon couple
   d a retired couple interested in the arts
   e you

3. Rewrite this postcard putting in punctuation and capital letters.

dear brandon

were having a great time here the weathers fantastic and there are lots of beautiful long sandy beaches we spend the days suntanning swimming and sailing and the evenings eating and drinking and dancing I hope youre well whats the weather like in Rochester

love crystal

49 Describing Places

Copacabana Beach, Rio de Janeiro, Brazil

The Golden Pavilion, Kyoto, Japan

St. Moritz, Switzerland

① Match these descriptions to the places above.

> Historical interest **Good for sports**
> An active holiday **A very relaxing place**
> **Ideal for families** PLENTY
> OF THINGS TO DO *Educational*
> Good for a short break
> **Expensive** **Too busy** Quiet
> GREAT FOR WINTER SPORTS
> *Lots of fun* **EXCITING** Great for
> swimming Tropical **IN THE**
> **MOUNTAINS** **fresh air**
> **HOT** cold **Beautiful**

② Listen to the three descriptions of vacations and answer these questions:

Max Devereux
a Where did Max go?
b Make a list of what he saw.

Natalie Trudeau
c Does Natalie like relaxing vacations?
d Where did she go?

Charlene Meeks
e What type of vacation is Charlene taking about?
f Which place does she remember the best? Why?

③ Describe the places shown above. Would you like to go there? Why?/ Why not?

④ Write a description of the place you went to for your last vacation. Include:

- how big the place is.
- the best season to visit it.
- how popular it is.
- what kind of people go there.
- the most important things to see.

50 Reserving an Airline Ticket

Read the conversation and then try to complete Nancy's sentences.
After, listen to the recording and compare.

Travel Agent: Good morning. Can I help you?
Nancy Lee: ....
....

Travel Agent: Hong Kong? Would that be a round trip ticket or one-way?
Nancy Lee: ....
Travel Agent: And for what date?
Nancy Lee: ....
Travel Agent: Friday, the eighteenth? Yes. That's fine. What about the return date? Do you have a fixed date in mind, or do you want an open ticket?
Nancy Lee: ....

Travel Agent: OK. Do you want a morning flight, or an afternoon flight?
Nancy Lee: ....
Travel Agent: Well, there's a Cathay Pacific flight at ten-thirty and a US Air one at twelve-thirty.
Nancy Lee: ....
Travel Agent: OK. If you'll just hold on a minute, I'll check to see if there's room. Yes, that's fine.
Nancy Lee: .... ?
Travel Agent: One thousand, eight hundred and seventy dollars.
Nancy Lee: ....
Travel Agent: Now, can I have your details, please?

1 **Listen again to the conversation. This time the recording only has the voice of the Travel Agent. You take the part of Nancy Lee.**

2 **Discuss in pairs:**

- In which class do you usually fly?
- What are the differences between the three main classes – First, Business and Economy?
- What's the difference between an open ticket and a restricted ticket?

Air Tickets

Open tickets cost you more. All **First** and **Business** class tickets are open. i.e. you can change your flight times. Full-fare **Economy** tickets are usually open.

Cheaper tickets are usually **Restricted**, i.e. you can't change them. The best known-type is **APEX** (Advance Purchase Excursion). Often you have to stay overnight - something most business travelers won't want to do!

Conversation A

Jessica Adams has called the *Worth The Earth* restaurant to reserve a table.

Hussein: Hello, this is Worth the Earth. Hussein speaking.

Jessica: Oh, hello. Do you have a table for a party of six, for tomorrow night?

Hussein: At what time?

Jessica: Eight-thirty.

Hussein: We're pretty busy tomorrow night. I have a table for nine o'clock, but not at eight-thirty.

Jessica: Nine o'clock will be fine. I just want to check something else. I haven't eaten there before, and I have a client who's a vegetarian. Do you have a vegetarian menu?

Hussein: No problem, ma'am. We have at least three vegetarian dishes on the menu every day.

Jessica: That's great.

Hussein: Party of six for nine o'clock. May I have your name, please?

Jessica: Jessica Adams.

Hussein: Fine. I'll see you tomorrow, Ms. Adams.

① Practice reserving a table for dinner next Thursday at 8:00.

② Michael Robertson is calling a theater to reserve tickets. Listen to the recording of his conversation (B) and complete the credit card slip for Jasmine.

③ In pairs, reserve five seats for a performance next Saturday. Pay with a credit card.

HUDSON THEATER: PHONE SALE: CUSTOMER NOT PRESENT

TYPE OF CARD: ☐ Visa ☐ Mastercard ☐ AmEx ☐ Diners Club

CARD MEMBER ACCOUNT NUMBER:

EXPIRATION DATE:

NAME AS PRINTED ON CARD:

AUTHORIZATION CODE (All sales over $200.00):

DATE OF CHARGES:

SEAT NUMBERS ASSIGNED:

TOTAL DEDUCTION:

FEDERAL U.S.A. CAR RENTAL ⊗

GRADE ECONOMY (E)
2 or 4 door
Sub-compact size.
Dodge Colt, Geo Metro or similar.
Air-conditioned with radio.
Allocated to singles, or two adults plus child.
Luggage space 5.6 cu. ft.
Weekly $126/Daily $34 (excluding C.D.W.)

GRADE COMPACT (C)
2 or 4 door
Compact size.
Dodge Shadow, Geo Prizm or similar with 4 seats.
Air-conditioned with radio.
Allocated to three adults, or two adults plus two children.
Luggage space 10.3 cu. ft.
Weekly $148/Daily $42 (excluding C.D.W.)

GRADE MID-SIZE (M)
Intermediate size.
Plymouth Acclaim, Lumina Euro Sedan or similar.
Air-conditioned with radio.
Allocated to four adults, or family with two older or three younger children.
Luggage space 12.3 cu. ft.
Weekly $164/Daily $46 (excluding C.D.W.)

GRADE FULL SIZE (F)
2 or 4 door
Full size.
Dodge Dynasty, Caprice Sedan or similar.
Air-conditioned with radio.
Five seats (six if you are friendly!)
Luggage space 15 cu. ft.
Weekly $198/Daily $52 (excluding C.D.W.)

GRADE CONVERTIBLE (G)
4 door
Convertible Chrysler Le Baron or similar.
4 seats. Suitable for two or three adults.
Air-conditioned with radio, electric roof.
Luggage space 10.3 cu. ft.
Weekly $304/Daily $70 (excluding C.D.W.)

GRADE STATION WAGON (S)
4 door
Station wagon.
5 seats.
Air-conditioned with radio.
Weekly $274/Daily $66 (excluding C.D.W.)

GRADE LUXURY (L)
4 door
Cadillac Sedan De Ville, Lincoln Town Car, or similar
Air-conditioned with radio
Power driver's seat. Leather upholstery
Luggage space: 12.1 cu.ft.
Weekly $298/Daily $70 (excluding C.D.W.)

GRADE LUXURY MINIVAN (V)
3 door
People carrier.
Plymouth Voyager Van, Chevrolet Lumina APV Van or similar.
Air-conditioned with radio.
7 seats but limited luggage space.
Weekly $304/Daily $76 (excluding C.D.W.)

Most cars are fitted with cruise control. All cars are automatic.

- We strongly recommend that C.D.W. (Collision Damage Waiver) should be added to all rentals at a cost of $10 per day for all vehicles.
- Personal accident insurance is $7 per day.
- Peak Season supplement: $20 per week per rental July 10th thru August 31st.
- Child seats on request: $3 per day.

Local State taxes (5% to 8%) not included in the rental rates. In Florida there will be an additional state surcharge of $2.05 per car per day. A full tank of fuel is provided and the car should be returned with a full tank.

---

1 Read through the car rental information above. Find out:

a the cheapest vehicle per day
b the most expensive vehicles per week
c the cost of one of the vehicles including C.D.W. per week in March
d the cost of the same vehicle including C.D.W. in late July
e the largest vehicle
f the vehicle with the smallest trunk
g the vehicle with the most seats
h the vehicle with the least space
i the extra daily tax you will have to pay in Florida
j the cost of a child seat per week

2 Ask another student questions using these patterns:

How much (luggage space) does it have?
How many (seats / doors) does it have?
Does it have (air conditioning / a radio / a cassette player)?
How big is the trunk?
How much will it be per (day / week / month)?
What make is a (grade E)?
Which car would you recommend?
Which car do you like best?
Which car would you rent?

53 Renting a Car

Natalie Trudeau is at the Federal-U.S.A. car rental office in the airport terminal.
Read the conversation and complete the sentences.
Then listen to the recording and compare.

Natalie: Good morning. I'd like ....
.... , please.
Clerk: Yes, ma'am. For .... ?
Natalie: For three days.
Clerk: All right. Where .... to
leave the car?
Natalie: .... leave it at the downtown office?
Clerk: Sure - you can .... our cars at any of
our offices. What kind of car ....
.... ?
Natalie: .... your brochure?
Clerk: ....
Natalie: Uh, it's not important really.
.... this one?
Clerk: OK. .... your driver's
license?

Natalie: I have an International Driver's License
and a French one.
Clerk: Fine. Thank you. Now, ...
C.D.W. and personal accident insurance?
Natalie: Sure. I'll take both.
Clerk: Right, can you check these two boxes, and
put your initials here, and again here.
Natalie: ....
Clerk: How do you want .... ?
Natalie: American Express, please.
Clerk: That's fine. Would you be interested in our
Federal Charge Card? It can be used at any
Federal Rental Office.
Natalie: I think I have too .... charge cards
already.

1 **Natalie Trudeau wants to rent a car for three days.
Notice that we say "for three days" but "until
Saturday". Write for or until in front of these words:**

....	Sunday	....	next month
....	July 14th	....	1999
....	two years	....	two weeks
....	Christmas Day	....	December
....	three days	....	twelve weeks

2 **In small groups, discuss:**

- Have you ever rented a car?
- Which company did you rent it from?
- Do you have a rental car company charge card?
- Where have you picked up and dropped off your
rental cars?
- Was it expensive to rent a car?
- Did/do you take car insurance (C.D.W.) when
renting a car?
- Have you ever had an accident in a rented car?

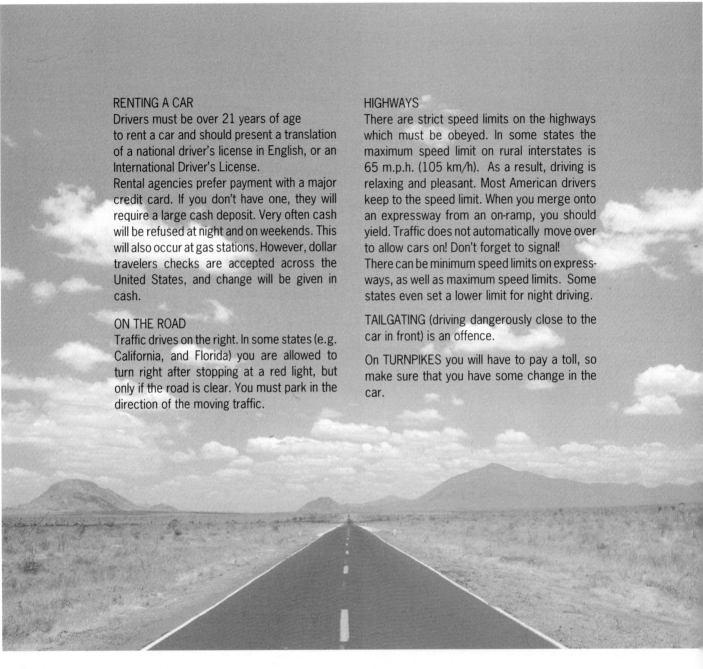

RENTING A CAR

Drivers must be over 21 years of age to rent a car and should present a translation of a national driver's license in English, or an International Driver's License.

Rental agencies prefer payment with a major credit card. If you don't have one, they will require a large cash deposit. Very often cash will be refused at night and on weekends. This will also occur at gas stations. However, dollar travelers checks are accepted across the United States, and change will be given in cash.

ON THE ROAD

Traffic drives on the right. In some states (e.g. California, and Florida) you are allowed to turn right after stopping at a red light, but only if the road is clear. You must park in the direction of the moving traffic.

HIGHWAYS

There are strict speed limits on the highways which must be obeyed. In some states the maximum speed limit on rural interstates is 65 m.p.h. (105 km/h). As a result, driving is relaxing and pleasant. Most American drivers keep to the speed limit. When you merge onto an expressway from an on-ramp, you should yield. Traffic does not automatically move over to allow cars on! Don't forget to signal!

There can be minimum speed limits on expressways, as well as maximum speed limits. Some states even set a lower limit for night driving.

TAILGATING (driving dangerously close to the car in front) is an offence.

On TURNPIKES you will have to pay a toll, so make sure that you have some change in the car.

---

1 **Read the above article.**

2 **True (✔) or False (✗) ?**

a ☐ You have to pay a toll on all expressways.
b ☐ Gas stations may not accept cash at night.
c ☐ No one obeys the speed limits.
d ☐ You can drive straight onto an expressway. The traffic will move over to let you in.
e ☐ You shouldn't drive too close to cars in front of you.

3 **Compare driving in the U.S.A. to driving in your country. Do you think you would find driving in the U.S.A. a problem? Why?/Why not?**

4 **Discuss these statements:**

- Men have more accidents than women, so they should pay more insurance.
- To conserve gas, there should be strict speed limits everywhere.
- People who drink and drive should go to jail.
- Everyone should re-take their driver's test every five years.
- There should be stricter speed limits for drivers under 21.

Ryan Thomas is in his office at WorldWide Entertainment in L.A. It's 5 o'clock in the afternoon. He has just asked to speak to Nathan Daniels from the Mail Room.

Ryan wants to send the following items:

- An urgent, two page letter to Consuela Rodriguez, who is visiting film companies in San Francisco.
- A sixty-page contract to Consuela's Head Office in Mexico City. It is urgent. They need it by the day after tomorrow.
- A different contract to WorldWide's New York office. He wants their lawyers to look at it. They will probably want to change some things in the document.
- A floppy disk to WorldWide's distributor in Taipei, Taiwan. It contains a list of films that WorldWide Entertainment distributes. The Taipei distributor wants to add Chinese translations to the list.
- A letter to the Frankfurt office. It needs to be there in one week's time.
- 100 catalogs to their Japanese distributor in Osaka. The distributor will not need them for two months.
- An informal postcard thanking their Frankfurt agent for his help during Ryan's recent visit.

These are the methods he could use to send the documents:

- Surface Mail. The cheapest. 2 to 6 weeks for international delivery.
- Airmail. Reasonably cheap. Allow 5 to 6 days for delivery.
- Express Mail. 2 to 3 days. $5 express charge in addition to postage.
- Courier. By private courier company. 36-48 hours for international delivery. Very expensive, but guaranteed.
- Fax. Instant. The price of a phone call. Doesn't look very formal. Not too good for long documents.
- E-Mail. Instant. The price of a phone call. Downloads a document from the sender's computer via a modem onto the recipient's computer. Ideal for sending documents that are (a) very urgent (b) need changing.

1 Read the information above and discuss the best way of sending the documents.

2 Listen to the recording, and write on the diagram the methods that were used, (e.g. *fax*).

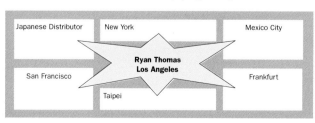

3 Complete this chart. Write four things you need to mail and the destination. Then discuss the best mail method.

Item	Destination	How urgent?	Method

Conversation A
At the Drug Store

Natalie Trudeau: Good morning. Do you have anything for a sore throat?
Pharmacist: How long have you had it?
Natalie Trudeau: It just started yesterday.
Pharmacist: Well, I recommend these antiseptic lozenges. They'll relieve the pain.
Natalie Trudeau: Thank you.
Pharmacist: But if it gets any worse, you should see your doctor.

Conversation B
Emergency dental treatment

Front Desk Clerk: How can I help you?
Consuela Rodriguez: I need a dentist. I've lost a filling.
Front Desk Clerk: How bad is it? There's a dentist down the road, but they're closed over the weekends.
Consuela Rodriguez: It's pretty painful! And, I'm traveling to L.A. tomorrow.
Front Desk Clerk: There *is* a 24-hour emergency dental service downtown. Wait here. I'll call them for you.

Conversation C
At the Medical Center

Wilbur Meeks: I'd like to see a doctor, please.
Nurse: Are you a regular patient here?
Wilbur Meeks: No, I'm just visiting the area.
Nurse: Can I ask you to complete this form? We'll need some information about you.

1 **Match the problems with the treatment.**

sore throat	after-sun lotion
headache	medicated lozenges
cold	antihistamine cream
a cut	decongestant
an insect bite	painkiller
sunburn	kaolin liquid
indigestion	antacid
upset stomach	Bandaid, antiseptic cream

2 **Look at Conversation A and the words in the box above. With a partner, practice similar conversations in a drug store.**

3 **In Conversation B look at the key words (in blue) and practice similar conversations:**

- chipped a tooth / a toothache / broken dentures
- down the street / uptown / on Birch Street
- today / on Sunday / this evening

4 **Read and listen to Conversation C. Then, complete the patient registration form for yourself.**

SUFFOLK COUNTY MEDICAL CENTER BOSTON		
Request for Emergency Treatment		
NAME		SEX
ADDRESS	street	
city	state	zip
TELEPHONE		
YOUR DOCTOR'S NAME & ADDRESS		street
city	state	zip
NAME OF NEXT OF KIN:		
KNOWN ALLERGIES TO DRUGS:		
PRE-EXISTING MEDICAL CONDITIONS:		
PRESENT COMPLAINT:		
Signature		Date

57 Hotel Problems

Conversation A
Wilbur Meeks has just arrived at the Studios Inn Hotel, in Hollywood. It's 12 noon.

Front Desk Clerk: Your room will be ready in approximately one hour, sir. We're getting it ready right now.
Wilbur: I'm sorry, this just isn't good enough! I want my room now. I've had a long flight from Chicago.
Front Desk Clerk: Our official check-in time is 3 p.m., Mr. Meeks. The departing guests don't have to check out until noon. I'm afraid we don't have a room available at the moment. If you'd like to take a seat in the bar. You can have a coffee while you're waiting.
Wilbur: I want to speak to the manager!

(Five minutes later)
Manager: … We're full because of the convention. I'm sorry, but there's nothing I can do.
Wilbur: Look, if I don't get a room now, I'll take my business elsewhere!
Manager: There's no need to get angry, Mr. Meeks. The room will be ready soon.
Wilbur: Don't you understand? I want it immediately!
Manager: Look here, Mr. Meeks. If you don't like our service, you might be happier elsewhere. I can call you a cab…

Conversation B
It's an hour earlier. Paul Washington is leaving the same hotel today.

Paul Washington: Oh, hello. Sorry to trouble you, but I wanted to ask about the check-out time.
Front Desk Clerk: It's twelve noon, Mr. Washington.
Paul Washington: Yes, I thought so. In that case, I wonder if you can do me a favor.
Front Desk Clerk: Sure. If I can.
Paul Washington: My flight doesn't leave until late this afternoon. Is there any possibility of an extended check-out time? I don't want to cause any problems. I'll understand if you can't do it.
Front Desk Clerk: Well, we're busy today … but I could give you an extra hour. Will that help?
Paul Washington: That's a big help. Thanks. 1 p.m., right?

1 In Conversation A there's a confrontation! The result is, Wilbur doesn't have a room, and the hotel has nearly lost a customer. Highlight the sentences in this conversation which helped to cause a confrontation.

2 Can you replace the words you highlighted with something more polite?

3 Listen to and read Conversation B. Highlight the things that Paul says which avoid a confrontation.

4 Now practice these situations again. But this time Wilbur is polite and Paul is angry.

58 Complaints

Natalie Trudeau: Hello. Front Desk?

Receptionist: Yes?

Natalie Trudeau: This is Natalie Trudeau in room 504.

Receptionist: Why, yes. How can I help you, Ms. Trudeau?

Natalie Trudeau: I want to take a shower and there's no hot water.

Receptionist: I can't understand that. Have you turned the handle all the way to the right?

Natalie Trudeau: I've been trying to get hot water for ten minutes! It's freezing cold.

Receptionist: Well, a lot of people take showers before breakfast. Maybe if you wait a while, it'll heat up again.

Natalie Trudeau: Wait! I have three appointments this morning, and I also have to wash and dry my hair.

Receptionist: You're sure there's absolutely no hot water?

Natalie Trudeau: No, none.

Receptionist: I'll contact maintenance and have them send someone up right away.

Natalie Trudeau: Who will that be?

Receptionist: The engineer.

Natalie Trudeau: Who's the engineer?

Receptionist: The engineer's the person who's responsible for all building maintenance. He'll be there within two minutes.

Natalie Trudeau: OK, but don't send anyone for five minutes! I'm still in my robe.

1 **Look at the key language (in blue). Make similar conversations, using these words:**

a housekeeper / cleaning rooms

b bell person / carrying luggage

c front desk manager / checking guests in and out

d room service waiter / bringing food to guests' rooms

e hotel operator / taking incoming and outgoing calls

2 **Phone front desk and complain about:**

a no towels

b no air conditioning

c TV out of order

d room service breakfast late

e noisy party next door

f insects in the bathroom

3 **Discuss:**

• Have you ever had to complain about something in a hotel? What happened? Were you satisfied?

• Have you ever had to complain about any other type of service or product, like service in a restaurant, or food from a store?

Natalie Trudeau is staying at the Presidential Standard Hotel, in Los Angeles. She doesn't like it very much. She found that the tub was dirty, the nightstand lamp didn't work, and the shower was cold. The air-conditioning was on full blast all night and her room's freezing. It's also very noisy and the service is bad. The restaurant is extremely expensive, and the food is very plain.

1 Natalie's at the Front Desk, to make a complaint in person.

Natalie Trudeau: Excuse me. I'm staying in room 504, and the air conditioner in my room won't turn off!

Front Desk Clerk: I'm so sorry Ms. Trudeau. I'll have it fixed right away.

Make similar conversations, using these words:

a shower / broken – fix
b tub / dirty – clean
c floor / dirty – vacuum
d nightstand lamp / broken – fix
e phone / out of order – repair
f mini bar / right out of mineral water – check and fill
g window / won't open – open

2 The Presidential Standard Hotel gives all guests a form to fill in, so that they can say what they think of the hotel. Fill in the form for Natalie Trudeau. Then compare it with others.

3 Discuss:

• What bad experiences have you had at hotels?
• What is the best hotel you have stayed in. Why?
• How often do you stay in hotels?
• Do you enjoy staying in hotels?

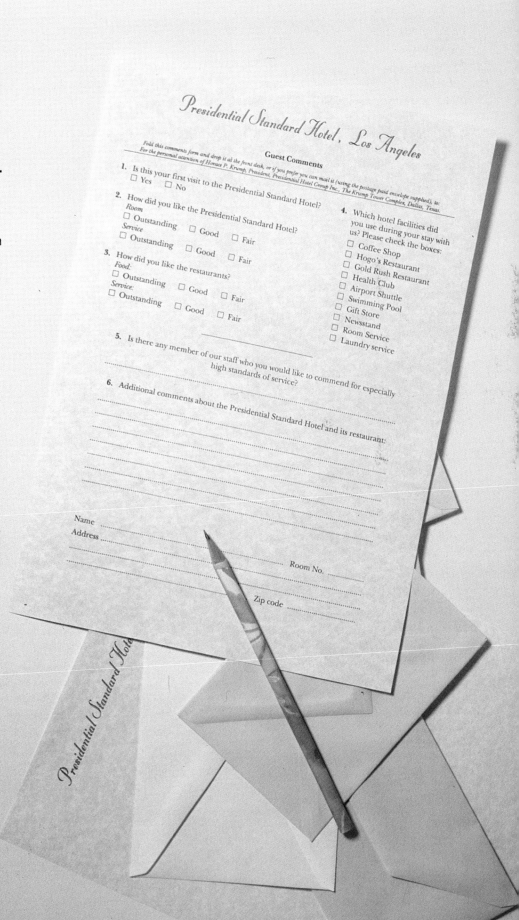

WEEKEND FLORIDA!
IN THE SUNSHINE STATE

Business trips often include weekends in the same place. What better place to be, than here in Tampa, Florida!

You can use this guide to explore the best that Florida has to offer. Invite a colleague along or a friend who knows the area. You'll have a great time!

SALVADOR DALI MUSEUM

The world's largest collection of works by the famous Spanish artist Salvador Dali.
Open Tues.– Sat. 10 – 5; Sun. 12 – 5.
Closed major holidays.
For rates and information call: (813) 823–3767
1000 Third Street South, St. Petersburg, FL.

BUSCH GARDENS, TAMPA

No place else can you experience in a single day the excitement of a Broadway-style show in a stately Moroccan Palace, explore the wilds of the Serengeti, feel the adventure of the Congo River, and shop the bazaars of Timbuktu! No place else but Busch Gardens at Tampa Bay on Florida's sunny west coast.
For recorded information call (813) 971-8282

EXCITEMENT YOU CAN GET YOUR HANDS ON! GREAT EXPLORATIONS

The Hands on Science Museum
Open 7 days a week   1120 4th Street South
Downtown St. Petersburg (813) 821–8885

THIS SUNDAY

National Football League
TAMPA BAY BUCCANEERS vs. ATLANTA FALCONS
Tampa Ticket Info. Hot line (813) 555–6392

TAMPA PAC CENTER
Call toll free: 1-800-544-9899

12th – 17th *The Phantom of the Opera*
Musical; Matinee & evening performances.
Tampa's PAC Festival Hall.

12th – 17th *Down in Dixie*
Satirical revue Tampa's PAC Playhouse

12th – 17th The Florida Orchestra
Concert: great movie themes.

CAUSEWAY TEN-SCREEN MULTIPLEX MOVIE THEATER

1 HOME ALONE AGAIN
2 TERMINATOR TEN
3 THAT MOUSE GOES SOUTH
4 NATIONAL LAUGHTER'S MOON VACATION
5 NIGHTMARE ON OAK BOULEVARD XIII
6 SLASH!
7 BULLMAN TWO
8 THE MAILMAN
9 LOST INHERITANCE
10 MUMBLE
(813) 007–5566

Rent-A-Boat

Rent a Mercury-powered boat and explore the islands off St. Petersburg beach – relax and suntan – fish – dive and enjoy all water sports
Contact Hank Wilson Charter, Clearwater, FL.

---

1 Ian King is in Tampa, and his business trip includes a weekend. He's deciding what to do. Read the guide to the Tampa area, above.
What would you do? Ask other people.

2 Find this information:

a the address of the Dali Museum
b the name of the boat rental company
c the title of the movie at Causeway Multiplex #4
d the cost of a phone call to Tampa's PAC Center
e the names of the football teams playing on Sunday

3 In pairs, suggest different things to do, using the expressions below.

Suggestion
Why don't we (go to a movie)?
Let's (go see a movie)!
Would you like to (go to a movie)?
How about (seeing a movie)?
What about (going to a movie)?
Do you want to (see a movie)?

Alternative ideas
I'd rather (go to the beach).
I'd prefer to (go to the beach).
How about (going to the beach) instead?
What about (going to the beach) instead?
Why don't we (go to the beach) instead?

61 Invitations

It's Friday afternoon, in Tampa, and Ian King is in a meeting with Rebecca Larsen and Leroy Allen.

Rebecca: So, we've agreed. We'll visit the factory site Monday morning.

Ian: That's fine with me.

Rebecca: Are you flying back to Atlanta for the weekend, Ian?

Ian: Um, no. I'm staying in Tampa.

Rebecca: Do you have any friends here?

Ian: No, but I don't know anyone in Atlanta, either.

Rebecca: Well, in that case, we can't leave you here on your own! Larry and I are taking our boys to the Salvador Dali Museum tomorrow. Why don't you join us? We can go to Busch Gardens in the afternoon. It's a theme park.

Ian: Oh, no, I couldn't. I'm sure you need a weekend break with your family.

Rebecca: Of course you can! I insist!

Ian: Well … if it's not too much trouble.

Rebecca: We'll pick you up at your hotel at 9:15? OK?

Ian: OK. Thank you very much.

Leroy: Hey, Ian. Have you ever seen an American football game?

Ian: Only on TV.

Leroy: How about coming along with me on Sunday? I'm going to see the Tampa Bay Buccaneers. They're playing the Atlanta Falcons.

Ian: Atlanta? I won't know which team to support!

Leroy: That's OK. I'll tell you!

Ian: I don't like to intrude on your weekend.

Leroy: No, I really mean it. It'll be great. I'll come and pick you up at your hotel late Sunday morning. Eleven o'clock? I'll show you the sights of Tampa before the game.

Ian: That sounds great. You're both very kind.

Leroy: We'll enjoy it.

① The two invitations are highlighted. Find and highlight these things:

a At first, Ian refuses both invitations. Highlight the refusals.

b After Ian refuses, both Rebecca and Leroy stress that they mean the invitation. Highlight what they say.

c Highlight Ian's thanks.

② Try inviting each other to:

a dinner on Sunday night
b an opera
c a moonlight dinner cruise
d a sumo wrestling fight

Don't forget, you may not want to go!

Invitations

Invitations are always a problem! People usually refuse the *first* invitation, in case the person inviting is only being polite. If you're inviting someone (and you really mean it!) you should expect to ask twice. Americans sometimes say that British people refuse three, four or even more times before accepting an offer or invitation!

62 Agreeing and Disagreeing

Conversation A
Wilbur Meeks is at a party with Mr. Devereux. He agrees with everything Mr. Devereux says.

Wilbur Meeks: Would you like a whiskey, sir?
Mr. Devereux: No, thanks – I .... whiskey.
Wilbur Meeks: Oh, neither do I, sir. How about a cigarette?
Mr. Devereux: No, thanks – I .... smoke anymore.
Wilbur Meeks: Oh, ... , sir. Nasty habit.
Mr. Devereux: Hmm, I .... these sandwiches.
Wilbur Meeks: Oh, so do I, sir!

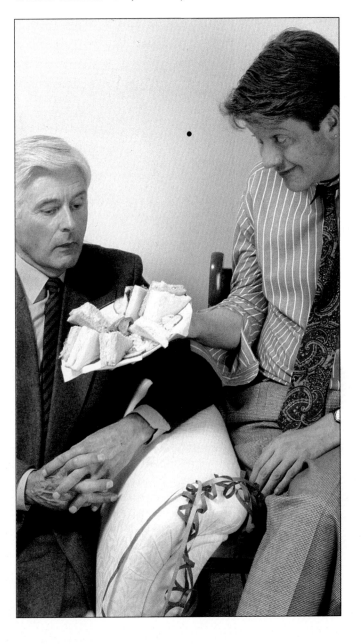

Conversation B
Wilbur Meeks is in a marketing meeting.

Mr. Devereux: The thing is, our new word processor needs more advertising.
Wilbur Meeks: ....
Mr. Devereux: The question is, what kind of advertising? Now, I've thought a lot about this, and I think we should try a television campaign.
Wilbur Meeks: ....
Mr. Devereux: A good TV campaign could increase sales by 50%.
Wilbur Meeks: ....
....
Mr. Devereux: I'm glad you agree, Wilbur. What about you, Linda?
Linda Foster: I'm afraid I don't agree, sir.
Mr. Devereux: What do you mean?
Linda Foster: In my opinion, it's a complete waste of money.
Wilbur Meeks: ....
– think of all the people who are going to see it.
Linda Foster: They might see it, but will they buy it?
Wilbur Meeks: Yes, I'm sure they will.
Linda Foster: I don't know. Think about it. We're talking about a $630 word processor, not a $29 Nintendo game! This is a serious business tool. We should advertise in the specialist business press!

1 **Look at these examples:**

Statement	Agree	Disagree
I like that album.	So do I!	I don't.
I don't like whiskey.	Neither do I!	I do.

Complete Conversation A and then compare your version to the recording.

2 **Look at Conversation B. Complete Wilbur's sentences, then listen to the recording and compare.**

3 **Which sports / foods / music / celebrities do/don't you like? Agree and disagree with your partner.**

Have you ever seen an ad for a Ferrari on TV?

Probably not. You won't find ads for laundry detergent in the financial magazines either. Advertisers have to choose their medium (e.g. TV, radio, magazines, newspapers, street advertising) carefully.

Millions of people see a TV commercial. How many of them have enough money to buy a Ferrari? Even in wealthy communities like Aspen, Colorado or Newport, Rhode Island only a tiny percent of people have the cash for a Ferrari. Maybe only 0.01% of the TV audience has enough money for that kind of luxury! On the other hand, nearly all of us buy laundry detergent.

TV commercials cost lots of money, and a specialist magazine or a serious newspaper doesn't sell space cheaply. Therefore, the important thing for an advertiser is to target the ad effectively.

When advertisers target an ad, they divide the population into six target groups, based on income and interests. This is an example:

Group A	Upper management Top professional
Group B	Middle management Skilled health workers Teachers
Group C1	White collar: office workers technicians
Group C2	Blue collar: industrial workers manual workers
Group D	Unskilled workers
Group E	Senior citizens Students Teenagers Children

1. **With a dictionary, look up the words in the article which you don't understand.**

2. **Which target groups do you think might read the publications in the picture?**

3. **Market researchers advise advertisers on how to reach the maximum audience for their products. Where would you advertise the following?**

shampoo	margarine	a $630 word processor
a stereo system	a TV set	a Nintendo game
tires	a daily newspaper	lawn mower
airline travel	a sports magazine	
beer	a rock CD	

4. **Role-play a marketing meeting. Choose a company president, a market researcher, and an advertising manager. Discuss together where you would advertise the items listed in Question 3.**

64 Giving Opinions

Frank: Yes, Naomi – I had a terrible time getting here – the city buses are on strike again.

Naomi: Yes, I know.

Frank: That's what's wrong with this country. Strikes should be forbidden. What do you think, Grant?

Grant: ....
....

Naomi: Well, if working conditions are bad, they have a right to strike. Don't you agree, Grant?

Grant: ....
....

Frank: It's a question of productivity, though. City and state workers are the laziest you'll find. Isn't that right, Grant?

Grant: ....
....

Naomi: That's an outrageous point of view, Frank. There are a lot of people out there on the city pay roll doing a really fine job. Isn't that so, Grant?

Grant: ....
....

Frank: What this country needs is longer hours and harder work – less leisure, less TV, and more work, eh, Grant?

Grant: ....
....

Naomi: Longer hours won't help the unemployed. Most of these people want to work, but they can't get jobs. Isn't this true, Grant?

Grant: ....
....

1 **Look at these expressions:**

Making your point
In my opinion / view …
I think / feel / believe that …
If you ask me … / As far as I'm concerned …

Introducing your ideas (when you disagree)
I see your point but …
I understand what you're saying, but …
You have a good point there, but …
I respect your opinion, but …

2 **Use the expressions in Question 1 to help you complete Grant's sentences. Then listen to the recording and take the part of Grant.**

3 **What are your opinions? Look at these statements and discuss:**

- Smoking should be banned in all public places.
- Parents should not hit their children to discipline them.
- There should be no capital punishment.
- There should be free trade between all countries.
- Medical services should be free.
- The whale trade and the fur trade should be banned permanently.
- We need urgent international agreement to save the atmosphere.
- Richer countries have a responsibility to help poorer countries.

The Sixth International Convention of Civil Engineers is being held at the Convention Center of the Studios Inn Hotel in Hollywood.

KEY

1   Paramount Suite
2   Ladies Rest Room
3   Exhibtion Hall
4   Main Entrance
5   Registration
6   Archway
7   Stairs
8   Gardens Restaurant
9   Universal Suite
10 Men's Rest Room
11 Main Hall
12 Convention Secretary

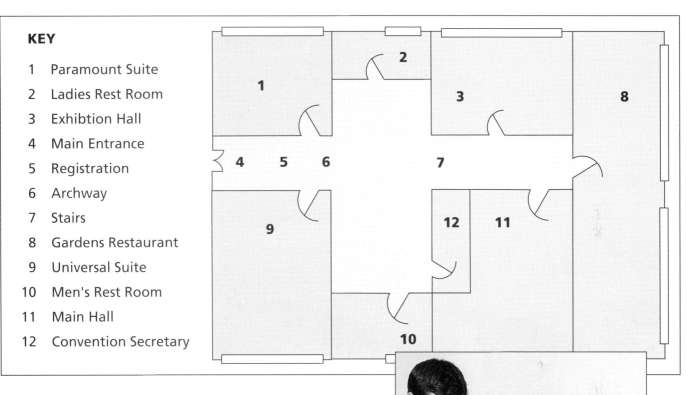

1 Listen to the three conversations and complete the chart.

	Name	Organization	Category	Color of pass
A				
B				
C				

2 Michael Robertson asked Sophie some questions at Registration. Here are the answers. What are the questions?

a   **Michael Robertson:** ....?
  Sophie: Sure. Go through the archway, down the stairs, and it's on the left.

b   **Michael Robertson:** ....?
  Sophie: Sure. Go through the archway, down the stairs, and it's straight ahead.

c   **Michael Robertson:** ....?
  Sophie: Sure. Go through the archway, down the stairs, and it's on the right.

3 With a partner, ask for and give directions around the Convention Center.

66 Making Plans

Dr. Santos is attending the Sixth International Convention of Civil Engineers. He has just registered.

Dr. Santos: Excuse me, ... where the Convention Secretary's office is?

Sophie: Sure. Go down the hall, turn right, and it's the first door on your left.

Dr. Santos: Thank you. Now – what did she say? .... I'll find his door .... Oh, here it is. James McGovern – Convention Secretary.

James McGovern: Come in!

Dr. Santos: Good morning. .... Dr. João Santos.

James McGovern: Well, Dr. Santos, it's a pleasure to ....

Dr. Santos: I understand you .... me to .... a speech tonight.

James McGovern: Yes, ... the best person to do it.

Dr. Santos: You .... me to .... the Japanese Ambassador.

James McGovern: That's right.

Dr. Santos: And how long .... me to .... ?

James McGovern: Oh, about ten or fifteen .... You .... a warm welcome in the name of the engineering profession and perhaps say .... about the purpose of the convention.

Dr. Santos: Sure, I can do that.

James McGovern: That's great. I'll leave it to you, then.

Dr. Santos: All right. .... and prepare ....

James McGovern: Fine. .... at dinner.

Dr. Santos: ....

① **Read the conversation above and complete the sentences. Then, listen to the recording and compare.**

② **Take turns being the convention secretary and have conversations for these situations:**

  a You want someone to speak for two or three minutes, thanking the convention organizers at the dinner.

  b You want someone to give a three hour presentation on word processing for a group of computer research scientists from a university in Nagoya.

  c You want someone to speak for ten minutes at an end of convention round table on "Engineering in the 21st century".

③ **Discuss in small groups:**

- Do you ever have to give speeches or presentations?
- How much preparation do you do?
- How do you feel when presenting to an audience?

67 Preparing a Speech

Read this conversation, and complete the sentences. Then listen to the recording and compare. Dr. Santos is in his room. James McGovern's secretary arrives.

Dr. Santos: Come in!
Linda Perez: Dr. Santos? .... Linda Perez, James McGovern's secretary. I'm typing up your speech from the micro-cassette, and I had a few questions.
Dr. Santos: Oh, come in, Ms. Perez - ah, ... call you Linda?
Linda Perez: Of course, Doctor.
Dr. Santos: Yes, well now, what .... ?
Linda Perez: How about I play through your tape and stop it where I have a question?
Dr. Santos: All right.
Tape (of Dr. Santos): Your Excellency, Mr. Chairman, Gentlemen –
Linda Perez: Yes, this is the .... one. I .... there will also be several women present.
Dr. Santos: Women? Oh, yes – then change it to ....
Linda Perez: All right.
Tape: I have great pleasure in .... today on behalf of our association –
Linda Perez: Ah, yes. .... the .... one. Um, there are two associations represented at the convention, aren't there?
Dr. Santos: Oh, yes, I'd forgotten about the North American Hydraulic Engineering guys. We'd .... that to "our associations".

Linda Perez: .... , Dr. Santos.
Tape: – and we are honored today by the presence of His Excellency, the Ambassador of Japan, who has .... over 5000 miles especially to be present at this, the Sixth International Convention of Civil Engineers.
Linda Perez: Here we are. Um, I .... it's less than 3000 miles from Washington D.C. to L.A.
Dr. Santos: Oh, right! I originally put kilometers. Thank you. Change it to "who has traveled .... especially to be present at this, the Sixth International Convention of Civil Engineers". How .... the speech sound to you, Linda?
Linda Perez: ...., Dr. Santos. I'm sure everyone will be ....

Notice how Linda introduces her corrections. She doesn't say, "That's wrong" or "It isn't right". She first says "I think" or "I believe".

1 **Devereux Computers hosted a cocktail party during the convention. Mr. Devereux asked Wilbur Meeks to formally introduce the guest of honor, Dr. Santos. Dr. Santos is a specialist in C.A.D. (Computer Assisted Design) from the University of Brasilia, and has helped to prepare a new C.A.D. program for Devereux.**

   Read the beginning of Wilbur's speech and correct it using the same methods as Linda Perez.

2 **In pairs, prepare notes about the other person, then introduce them to the class. What do they do? Where are they from? What are their qualifications? What are they going to talk about?**

DEVEREUX COMPUTERS INC.

I have the greatest honor and pleasure in introducing Mr. John Sanchez from the University of Brazil, which is in Rio de Janeiro. Professor Sanchez, as many of you know, has come over 10,000 miles to be here with us in Seattle. He is a specialist in C.A.L.L., that's Computer Assisted Language Learning to those who don't know anything about computers, but if you don't know anything about computers you shouldn't be here! (pause here for audience laughter, 30 seconds, I hope). John - if I may call him John - is a great programmer and helped to program our new C.A.L.L. package.

68 Convention Planner

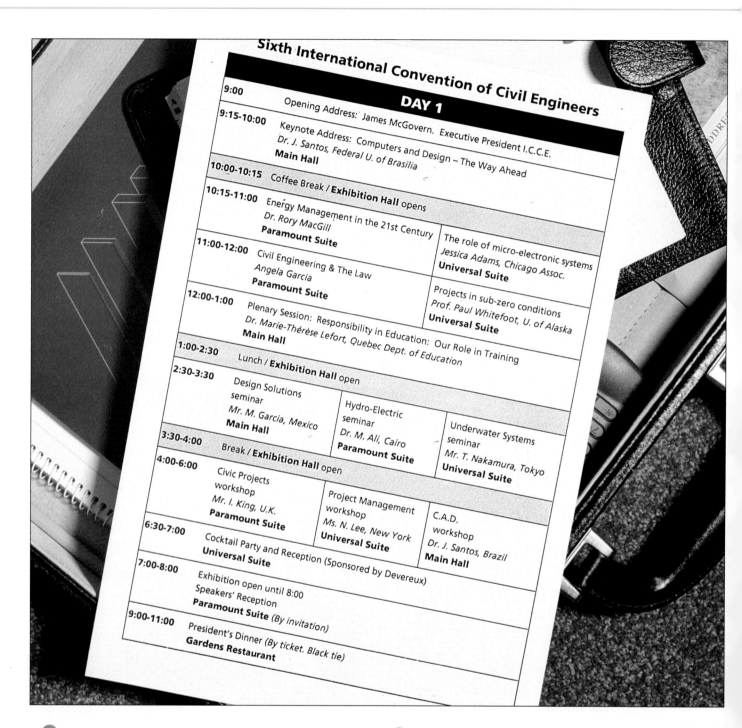

Sixth International Convention of Civil Engineers
DAY 1

9:00	Opening Address: James McGovern. Executive President I.C.C.E.		
9:15-10:00	Keynote Address: Computers and Design – The Way Ahead Dr. J. Santos, Federal U. of Brasilia **Main Hall**		
10:00-10:15	Coffee Break / **Exhibition Hall** opens		
10:15-11:00	Energy Management in the 21st Century Dr. Rory MacGill **Paramount Suite**	The role of micro-electronic systems Jessica Adams, Chicago Assoc. **Universal Suite**	
11:00-12:00	Civil Engineering & The Law Angela Garcia **Paramount Suite**	Projects in sub-zero conditions Prof. Paul Whitefoot, U. of Alaska **Universal Suite**	
12:00-1:00	Plenary Session: Responsibility in Education: Our Role in Training Dr. Marie-Thérèse Lefort, Quebec Dept. of Education **Main Hall**		
1:00-2:30	Lunch / **Exhibition Hall** open		
2:30-3:30	Design Solutions seminar Mr. M. Garcia, Mexico **Main Hall**	Hydro-Electric seminar Dr. M. Ali, Cairo **Paramount Suite**	Underwater Systems seminar Mr. T. Nakamura, Tokyo **Universal Suite**
3:30-4:00	Break / **Exhibition Hall** open		
4:00-6:00	Civic Projects workshop Mr. I. King, U.K. **Paramount Suite**	Project Management workshop Ms. N. Lee, New York **Universal Suite**	C.A.D. workshop Dr. J. Santos, Brazil **Main Hall**
6:30-7:00	Cocktail Party and Reception (Sponsored by Devereux) **Universal Suite**		
7:00-8:00	Exhibition open until 8:00 Speakers' Reception **Paramount Suite** (By invitation)		
9:00-11:00	President's Dinner (By ticket. Black tie) **Gardens Restaurant**		

1 Before the convention

Student A: Imagine that you are responsible for computer design training at a large company. Circle the presentations you are going to attend.

Student B: Imagine that you are project manager for a company that builds underwater oil pipelines for use in Siberia. Circle the presentations you are going to attend.

Explain your choice(s) to each other.

2 At the end of the day

Listen to the recording of Michael Robertson speaking to Jessica Adams. Highlight on the planner the things he attended on the first day.

3 Discuss:

- Do you attend conventions / conferences / exhibitions?
- As a speaker / exhibitor / participant / presenter / organizer.
- Do you enjoy these events? Why? Why not?
- How valuable are they?

Studios Inn — SIH — Room Service

Available 24 hours a day. Press 8.

SANDWICHES

Studios Club Sandwich $9.95
Thinly-sliced ham, turkey, Wisconsin cheese, tomato, lettuce, mayo.

House Special Open-faced Sandwich $10.95
Avocado, bacon pieces, thinly-sliced turkey, cheese, blue cheese dressing
served with potato chips.

Studios Big Burger $12.95
12oz. 100% American beef, onions, tomato, jumbo dill pickle, ketchup, relish
served in sesame seed roll with french fries.

SALADS

Chef's Salad $14.95
Turkey, ham, beef, cheese, eggs, olives, green beans, avocado served on bed
of radicchio and romaine lettuce. Choice of six dressings - Thousand Island,
Blue Cheese, French, Italian, Yogurt, Classic (oil and vinegar).

Salad Nicoise $14.95
Tuna, anchovies, egg, olives, tomato, green beans, capers served on bed of
lettuce. Choice of dressings as above.

CHEF'S VEGETARIAN SPECIAL $14.95
Stir-fried market vegetables in soy sauce, served with tofu.

CHILDREN'S SPECIALS All $4.50 each
Pizza
Spaghetti with meatball sauce
B.L.T. and fries
Child's burger and fries

A room service charge of $5.00 per order will be added to all orders

1 Consuela Rodriguez has just returned to her room at the Studios Inn Hotel, after her trip to San Francisco. It's 11:30 p.m. She didn't eat anything on the flight, so she's decided to order something from Room Service. Listen to the recording. What did Consuela order?

2 Look at the menu. In pairs, order a room service meal for:

a a family with two children
b someone who wants a large meal
c a vegetarian
d yourself

3 When you are on a business trip, do you usually order from the hotel's room service, or do you eat in restaurants? Discuss.

4 When your company has out of town visitors, how are they looked after?

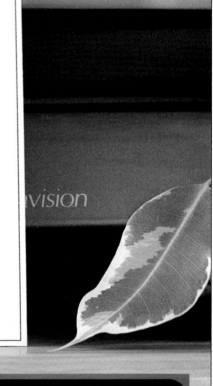

The Studios Inn Hotel has a TV check-out system. You can call up your room charge account at any time during your stay simply by pressing 33 on your TV remote control. Use the plus (+) button to scroll up, and the minus (-) button to scroll down. When you wish to check-out, you can review your account on screen, then simply press 44 to speak to Accounts so that you can confirm that you approve of the charge.

Room 743:	Ms. C. Rodriguez	PAGE 8
Method of payment:	Mastercard	
September 20	9:51 a.m.	

Carry over from previous pages:	$3,128.65

Room charge 9/19	170.00
Room service 9/19	18.95
Laundry service 9/19	13.25
Mini-bar 9/19	6.00
Internat. Telephone 9/19	15.37
Nat. Telephone 9/19	0.81
Buffet bkfst. 20/9	12.50
Business Services 20/9	56.05

Total for last 24 hours:	292.93
Grand total:	3,421.58
State tax at 18% on grand total:	615.88

Amount due:	$4,037.46

Room 843:	Mr. W. Meeks	PAGE 1
Method of payment:	Mail account to Devereax Computers, Seattle.	
September 20	9:51 a.m.	

Carry over from previous pages:	0.00

Room charge 9/19	170.00
Movie charge 9/19	39.00
Nat. Telephone 9/19	102.76
Mini-bar 9/19	198.56
Buffet bkfst. 20/9	75.00

Total for last 24 hours:	595.32
Grand total:	595.32
State tax at 18% on grand total:	107.16

Amount due:	$ 702.48

1 You are Consuela. You only had one $3.00 bottle of mineral water from the mini-bar. The international call is correct, but you made no other calls. You have forgotten that you also had a glass of wine with your room service meal. Call the accounts department and check the bill.

2 Listen to the recording of Wilbur Meeks trying to explain his room expenses to his boss, Max Devereux. List what went wrong.

3 Write out a room bill for your partner. Your partner disagrees with the charge.

4 Discuss:

- Have you ever used a TV check-out system?
- In the future do you think all check-ins / check-outs will be done on TV screens?
- Do you think TV check-out will be more efficient / more convenient / less personal / more accurate?

71 Survival!

Survival Challenge

Played in pairs.
One person is the traveler, the other person plays the other parts, ie. cab driver, company president. Decide on the route you want to take. Make brief conversations in each of the situations you've chosen. See if you can survive until the end.

Remember! In this Survival game, you must speak English! If you don't understand something, or need more time to think of an answer, use these phrases:

I'm sorry, I don't understand.
Could you repeat that.
Could you say that again more slowly.
Could you speak more slowly, please.

Check that you understand by repeating what your partner says. If you have a problem, go back to the lesson.
You can also use the Wordlist, and Grammar section to help you. Good luck! And have a good trip!

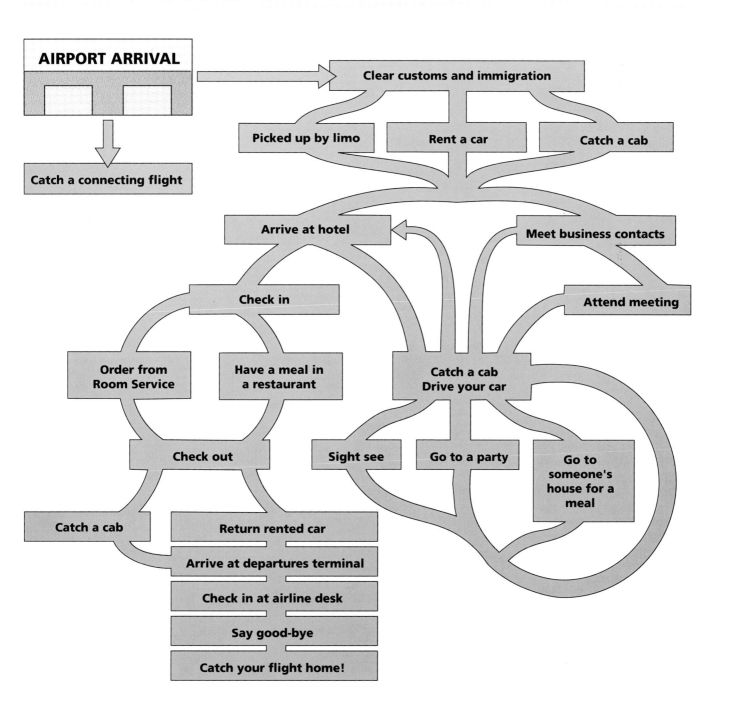

72 Good-Bye

Conversation A

Consuela Rodriguez: Well, good-bye, Ryan. Don't forget, ...

Ryan Thomas: I will. ....?

Consuela Rodriguez: Of course.

Ryan Thomas: ....

Consuela Rodriguez: Oh, yes. It was fine. Except for the last few days. It's been full of people for the Engineer's Convention!

Conversation B

Max Devereux: So, ... in Seattle.

Michael Robertson: Yes. I'll report back to my bosses in Toronto tomorrow, and ....

Max Devereux: I certainly think we can do business together, Michael.

Michael Robertson: I hope so.

Conversation C

Bell Captain: Excuse me! Mr. Meeks!

Wilbur Meeks: Ah, yes?

Bell Captain: The Front Desk Manager wants to speak to you before you leave, sir.

Wilbur Meeks: ....

Bell Captain: .... sir. There's something about a cleaning charge for your carpet …

Conversation D

James McGovern: Thank you again, Dr. Santos. .... And thank you for your impressive speech!

João Santos: Well, ...

James McGovern: That's what I'm here for.

João Santos: Well, ... Good-bye.

1 Read the conversations and complete the sentences, using the expressions from the box below. Then listen to the recording and compare.

> **Expressions:**
> … it's been nice to meet you.
> I'll call your secretary to arrange a meeting.
> I'll look forward to seeing you
> I'm in a hurry. I have a plane to catch.
> … if you're ever in Mexico City, you should come and see us.
> … thank you for all your help.
> And we'll see you again next year?
> It's been a pleasure having you here,
> It will only take a moment.
> I hope the hotel was OK.

2 Collect business cards or addresses from the people in your class who you want to keep in touch with. Here are some phrases to help:

Do you have a card? Here's my card/address.
Would you like my card/address?
May I have your card/address?

3 Say good-bye to each other using these words to help:

It's been nice to meet you. Good to meet you.
I enjoyed getting to know you. See you again.
See you soon. Take care. Bye. Good-bye. Keep in touch.

Grammar Reference

Grammar point	Survival File
Adjectives	16
Adverbs	17
Adverbs of frequency	3, 17
ago	6
allowed to	7
any	15
Be	1
can	8
Comparatives	16
Conditional sentences **see *if***	
could	8
Countable & uncountable nouns	15
'd **see *would* or *had***	
did (+ infinitive)	6
do/does (+ infinitive)	3
do/does have	2
do/does have to	7
ever (have you ever?)	5
few	15
for	5
Future continuous	4
Future simple	4
Future tenses	4
Gerunds	12
going to	4
got	2
Have	2
have/has been doing	5
have/has done	5
have/has (got)	2
have/has (got) to	7
have something done	11
had better	7
How?	9
How about?	9
How? + adjectives	9
How long?	5, 9
How much/many?	9, 15
How often?	9
if sentences	10
Infinitive	12
Irregular verbs	18
just (have just done)	5
'll **see *will***	
least	16
less	16
little	15
lot of	15
many	15
may	8

Grammar point	Survival File
might	8
Modals	7, 8
more	16
most	16
much	15
must	7
need	7
Passive	11
Past continuous	6
Past simple	6
Past tenses	6
Phrasal verbs	13
Perfect tenses	5
Prepositions	13, 14
Present continuous	3
Present perfect continuous	5
Present perfect simple	5
Present simple	3
Present tenses	3
Quantities	15
Questions	9
should	7
since	5
some	15
Superlatives	16
there is/are	1
there was/were	1
used to do	6
Verbs with prepositions	13
Want someone to do	12
What?	9
What about?	9, 12
What kind of?	9
What . . . like?	9
What make?	9
What type of?	9
When?	9
Where?	9
Which?	9
Who?	9
Whose?	9
Why?	9
will be doing	4
will have to	8
will (+ infinitive)	4, 8
would like	8
would like someone to do	12
would you mind	12
yet (haven't done yet)	5

Color Code:

Affirmative/Negative	Question	Short Answer

SURVIVAL FILE 1: *Be*

A Present

I	am	
	'm	
	'm not	
You	are	
We	're	from Winchester. (Unit 1)
They	aren't	
He	is	
She	's	
It	isn't	

Am	I	
Are	you	here on business? (Unit 1)
Is	she	

Yes, I am.	No, I'm not.
Yes, she is.	No, we aren't.
Never shortened	**Always** shortened

The affirmative is usually shortened. You can also say **you're not** etc, in the negative.

B Past

I		
He	was	
She	wasn't	
It		in Norfolk. (Unit 1)
You	were	
We	weren't	
They		

Was	he	
Were	they	in the air force? (Unit 1)

Yes, I was.	No, she wasn't.
Yes, it was.	No, we weren't.

C *There is …*

There are three Sheratons in Atlanta. (Unit 1)

Is there any pecan pie? (Unit 13)

There were lots of schoolkids at all of the temples. (Unit 49)

Was there much to do? (Unit 48)

> For other tenses of *be*, follow the rules in Survival Files 4 and 5.

SURVIVAL FILE 2: *Have*

A

I		
You	have	
We	don't have	
They		an appointment
He	has	with Ms. Adams.
She	doesn't have	(Unit 3)
It		

Do	you	have	satellite TV? (Unit 8)
Does	it		

Yes, I do.	No, we don't.
Yes, it does.	No, it doesn't.

1. To express possession.
   I only **have** 50 dollars. (Unit 32)
   Does Jacob Fielding **have** dark hair? (Unit 42)

2. In expressions when you mean **eat, drink, wear, experience, take …**
   I'll have the Chef's Salad, please. (Unit 69)
   We had a good time. (Unit 49)

B You can also say:

I			
You	've		
We	haven't		
They		got	ice-cream.
			(Unit 13)
He	's		
She	hasn't		
It			

Have	you	got	any green beans?
Has	he		(Unit 13)

Yes, I have.	No, we haven't.
Yes, he has.	No, she hasn't.

1. **Have got** is more common in Great Britain.
2. **Have got** only exists in the present tense.
3. You can only express possession with **have got**.

> For other tenses of *have*, follow the rules in Survival Files 3, 4, 5 and 6.

A Present simple

I		
You	work	
We	don't work	
They		in our Paris
He	works	office. (Unit 1)
She	doesn't work	
It		

Do	you	want	a roll with the meal?
Does	he		(Unit 13)

Yes, I do.	No, I don't.
Yes, he does.	No, he doesn't.

1. Something regular, a habit or something which is part of your life.
I work in our Paris office. (Unit 41)
Often with adverbs of frequency. (See **Survival File 17**)
In America, you **usually give** tips to waiters. (Unit 1)

2. Something you think or feel.
I love the fall. (Unit 28)
3. Regular times and schedules.
My flight **doesn't leave** until late this afternoon. (Unit 57)

B Present continuous

I	am		
	'm (not)		
You	're		
We	are	visiting	customers.
They	aren't		(Unit 11)
He	's		
She	is		
It	isn't		

Are	you	flying	back to Atlanta for
Is	he		the weekend?
			(Unit 61)

Yes, I am.	No, I'm not.
Yes, he is.	No, he isn't.

1. Something which is happening at the moment or a situation which changes. **She's really enjoying** Chicago. (Unit 10)
2. Something you have arranged to do in the future.
We usually say **when**. (See **Survival File 4**)
He's going to England **in January**. (Unit 3)

3. Some verbs are almost never in the continuous form. These are mostly verbs expressing feelings, mental activity and perception.
For example: like / love / hate / know / understand / want / see / hear / seem

A Future simple

I			
You	'll		
He	will		
She		get	ready in half an
It	won't		hour. (Unit 51)
We			
They			

Will	they	buy	it? (Unit 62)

Yes, they will.	No, they won't.

1. Something you say the moment you decide.
I'll take mashed potatoes. (Unit 13)
2. Something you think or hope will happen.
We hope you'll fly with us again soon. (Unit 18)
3. Future certainties: you are sure these will happen.
There will also **be** several women present. (Unit 67)

4. Something you offer, agree or promise to do, or something you ask or invite someone else to do. (See **Survival Files 7 and 8**)
I'll phone for some coffee. (Unit 2)
Will you follow me, please? (Unit 2)

B Going to (+ verb)

Use **going to** for something you plan to do or have already decided to do.
Where **is Jessica going to be** on Tuesday?
She's going to be in Tokyo. (Unit 4)
What is **Consuela going to eat**?

C Future continuous

In everyday situations, the **Future continuous** is very similar to the **Present continuous** or **going to** and used for something arranged or planned. (See **Survival File 3**)
Will you be paying by credit card? (Unit 8)
Our flight attendants **will be serving** lunch in a moment. (Unit 18)

SURVIVAL FILE 5: Perfect Tenses

A   Present perfect simple

| I
You
We
They | 've
have
haven't | | | |
| He
She
It | 's
has
hasn't | arrived | in Atlanta.
(Unit 1) | |

| Have | you | had | a vacation this year? | Yes, I have. | No, I haven't. |
| Has | she | | (Unit 48) | Yes, he has. | No, she hasn't. |

Regular verbs: the **past participle** takes **d** or **ed**.
arrive — arrive**d**   stay — stay**ed**

1. Past experiences usually with no indication of time. Often with
   ever or **never**.
   *I don't know him personally, but **I've spoken** to him on the phone.*
   (Unit 41)
   ***Have you ever been** to New Orleans?* (Unit 28)
2. When you can see the results of a recent event in the present.
   Often with **just, already** or **yet**.
   *I need a dentist. **I've just lost** a filling.* (Unit 56)
   *My bag **hasn't arrived yet**.* (Unit 33)

Irregular verbs: the **past participle** changes.
have — **had**   (see **Survival File 18**)

3. Events which started in the past and continue in the present.
   *How long **have you been** here?* (Unit 11)
   With **for** to say the length of time of the event.
   ***I've been** here **for** three days.* (Unit 11)
   With **since** to say when the event started.
   ***I've been** here **since** January.* (Unit 11)
4. Events which have happened in an unfinished period of time.
   ***I've been** to seven countries **this year**.* (Unit 38)

B   Present perfect continuous

The **Present perfect continuous** sometimes emphasizes the
continuous or repeated nature of the event. (See 3 above)
*How long **have** you **been living** in Seattle?* (Unit 20)
***I've been trying** to get hot water **for** 10 minutes.* (Unit 58)

Don't forget that certain verbs in English almost never take the continuous form. (See **Survival File 3**)

SURVIVAL FILE 6: Past Tenses

A   Past simple

I You He She	mixed			
	didn't mix	business with pleasure. (Unit 49)		
It We	met	Paul last year. (Unit 41)		
They	didn't meet			

| Did | he | know | Wilbur well? (Unit 19) | Yes, he did. | No, he didn't. |

Regular verbs: add **d** or **ed** in the affirmative.
mix — mix**ed**   arrive — arrive**d**

Irregular verbs: change in the affirmative.
meet — **met**   (see **Survival File 18**)

1. Use for a past completed event with no link to the present. There is often an indication of when it happened.
   ***We went** down to Kyoto **after I finished doing business in Tokyo**.* (Unit 49)
2. If there is no date, it is because it is understood or already established.
   ***We stayed** in a traditional Japanese hotel, a Ryokan.* (Unit 49)
3. You often use ... **ago** and **last** ... .
   ***I got** here two days **ago**.* (Unit 11)
   ***Last year** they **lost** my suitcase.* (Unit 33)

B   *Used to*

A past situation, habit, or something you did regularly in the past. Now, it's finished.
***I used to work** in the London office, then in Boston.* (Unit 20)
(I didn't use to work ... .   Did you use to work ... ?)

C   Past continuous

Something in progress at a certain time in the past. You don't know when the action started or finished.
***I was looking** at that sweater in the window.* (Unit 22)
***They were talking** together.*

The **Modal Verbs** *have to*, *must*, *need*, *allowed to*, *should*, *had better*, are mostly used in the following situations:

1. **Obligation**

   I *have to* wash and dry my hair. (Unit 58)
   You'*ll have to* report to the Transfer Desk in Denver. (Unit 15)

2. **Necessity**

   What do you *need*? (Unit 27)
   I'*ll need* some small bills. (Unit 24)

3. **Something prohibited**

   Passengers *must not* take off their seat belts. (Unit 18)
   You'*re not allowed to* take any alcohol to Saudi Arabia. (Unit 32)

4. **Advice/recommendation**

   You *should* see your doctor. (Unit 56)
   You'*d better* write one. (Unit 33)

5. **No obligation/necessity**

   It *doesn't have to* go through the scanner. (Unit 16)
   You *won't have to* pick it up in Denver. (Unit 15)
   There's *no need to* get angry. (Unit 57)
   You *don't need to* change them. (Unit 24)

The **Modal Verbs** *can, could, may, might, will, would,* are mostly used in the following situations.

1. **Possibility**

   A good TV campaign *could* increase sales by 50%. (Unit 62)
   (Future Possibility)
   Your insurance company *might* ask for an itemized list. (Unit 33)

2. **Asking for something**

   Can I ask you something, Dave? (Unit 5)
   Could I see the wine list? (Unit 12)
   May I see some identification? (Unit 24)

3. **Permission/Ability**

   You *can* go through. (Unit 16)
   I'm afraid you *can't* use that here. (Unit 17)
   I hope you *can* get it clean. (Unit 21)

4. **Asking someone to do something**

   Will you follow me, please? (Unit 2)
   Would you sign in, please? (Unit 26)
   Can you get me a Denver newspaper? (Unit 17)
   Could you call me a cab, please? (Unit 25)

5. **Promising/Agreeing**

   I'*ll* bring it right away. (Unit 12)
   Yes, I'*ll* take two packs of that gum, too. (Unit 7)

6. **Making Offers/Expressing preferences**

   What kind of room *would you like*? (Unit 8)
   I'*d like* a table for one, please. (Unit 12)

SURVIVAL FILE 9: Questions

1. To make a question you usually put the correct auxiliary verb (e.g. **be, have, do**), before the subject of the sentence. Don't just change the intonation of an affirmative sentence.

*When **did you get** here? (Unit 11)*
*What **can I do** for you? (Unit 24)*
*Where **are you going**? (Unit 25)*

2. Prepositions often go at the end of questions.

*Hey, where are you **from**? (Unit 1)*
*Who did you go **with**? (Unit 48)*

3. What?, Which?, Whose? and **How much/many?** are often followed directly by objects or phrases.

***What kind of room** would you like? (Unit 8)*
***What make** is a Grade E? (Unit 52)*
***Which types of hardware** do you most use? (Unit 47)*
***Whose office** was it? (Unit 19)*
***How much money** would you like? (Unit 24)*

4. How? and **What ... like?** are used to ask for a description of something. **How + be** is also used for health.

***How** was the traffic from the airport? Pretty awful! (Unit 2)*
***What's** your room **like**? Very nice. (Unit 9)*
***How's** Jodie? She's fine. (Unit 10)*

5. Many **adjectives** and **adverbs** are used after **How?** to ask about size, frequency, etc.

length of time/duration	***How long** will you be staying in the States? (Unit 10)*
frequency	***How often** do you stay in hotels? (Unit 59)*
size	***How big** is the trunk? (Unit 52)*
degree of popularity	***How popular** is it? (Unit 49)*
value	***How valuable** are they? (Unit 68)*

SURVIVAL FILE 10: *If* Sentences

The **1st Conditional** is used for a situation with **probable result**. It is usually formed like this:

If	**+**	**present tense**	➡	**future tense**
If		*you **don't have** a major credit card,*		*they **will require** a large cash deposit. (Unit 5)*
If		*you **wait** a while,*		***it'll heat** up again. (Unit 58)*
If		*I **don't get** a room now,*		***I'll take** my business elsewhere. (Unit 57)*

Other uses:

Situation with a **possible result**

If	**+**	**present tense**	➡	**may, might, can, could**
If		*you **don't like** our service,*		*you **might be** happier elsewhere. (Unit 57)*

Situation where you're **advising** or **instructing**

If	**+**	**present tense**	➡	**should, imperative**
If		*you**'re** ever in Mexico City,*		*you **should come** and see us. (Unit 72)*
If		*you **want** to enquire about reservations,*		***press** 'two' now. (Unit 31)*

Situation where you're giving a **normal reaction** to something

If	**+**	**present tense**	➡	**present tense**
If		*working conditions **are** bad,*		*they **have** a right to strike. (Unit 64)*

When you're **asking someone politely** to do something

If	**+**	**future tense**	➡	**present or future tense**
If		*you**'ll excuse** me,*		***I have to** go. (Unit 10)*
If		*you**'ll** just **hold** a minute,*		***I'll check** to see if there's room. (Unit 50)*

1. To form the **Passive**, use the verb **be** and add the **Past participle.** (See **Survival File 18** for Irregular Verbs)

It   is
           was
           has been
           will be
           can be
           is being

                        done / said /made / etc.

They   are
           were
           have been
           are being

Present	*Is it sold* by the glass? (Unit 12)
Past	*Was it lost* forever or *was it found?* (Unit 33)
Can	*It can be used* at any Federal Rental office. (Unit 53)
Present &	*Dollar travelers checks are accepted* across the United States
Future	and change *will be given* in cash. (Unit 54)
Should	*Smoking should be banned* in all public places. (Unit 64)

2. Use the **Passive** in the **Past simple** with **born.**

*Where was **he born**?* (Unit 5)
***She was born** in 1961.* (Unit 5)

3. When someone does something for you, but it isn't important *who* does it, you can use the **Passive** expression **have, want** or **would like** something **done.**
***I'll have it fixed** right away.* (Unit 59)
*How do you **want it sent**?* (Unit 55)

A Gerund (verb + *ing*)

1. After all prepositions. (Also after verbs and expressions taking prepositions.)

*Thank you **for inviting** us.* (Unit 21)
***What about going** to a movie?* (Unit 60)

Be careful with **to**. Sometimes it's a preposition. Sometimes it's part of the infinitive.

*I'll look forward **to seeing** you.* (Unit 30)
*I'd like **to use** the pool.* (Unit 26)

2. When a verb becomes the subject of a sentence.

*But **selling** is selling.* (Unit 38)
***Tailgating** is an offence.* (Unit 54)

3. After certain verbs and expressions.

*Is it **worth using** computer graphics?* (Unit 45)
*Would you **mind opening** your briefcase?* (Unit 16)

4. Some social expressions take either the gerund or the infinitive.

*It's **nice to meet** you.* (Unit 10)
*It was **nice meeting** you.* (Unit 10)

B Infinitive

Use the infinitive after **want, would like, ask** and **prefer** when you want someone else to do something.

*Can I **ask you to complete** this form?* (Unit 56)
*I just **wanted you to look** at page ten in the brochure.* (Unit 28)

SURVIVAL FILE 13: Verbs with Prepositions

1. Some verbs need prepositions. The verbs do not change meaning.

agree with (Unit 62)
apologize for (Unit 18)
ask for (Unit 33)
charge to (Unit 27)
explain about (Unit 28)
feel about (Unit 28)
hear about (Unit 20)
look at (Unit 12)
look for (Unit 39)

pay by (Unit 8)
pay for (Unit 33)
sell by (Unit 12)
talk about (Unit 28)
thank for (Unit 44)
think about (Unit 32)
think of (Unit 11)
wait for (Unit 33)
write out (Unit 70)

*I hate **waiting for** baggage, don't you?* (Unit 33)
*First, I wanted to **thank** you **for** all your help.* (Unit 44)

2. With verbs of movement, the direction is shown by the preposition, not the verb.

 go across (Unit 36)

go (straight) ahead (Unit 36)

 go down (Unit 36)

 go past (Unit 36)

go through (Unit 16)

 go up (Unit 36)

take into (Unit 32)

 take up to (Unit 8)

3. When the verb changes meaning completely because of the preposition, it is called a **Phrasal Verb**. Look at this list of common Phrasal Verbs.

be out of (Unit 17)	have no more of
check in (Unit 8)	register your arrival
check out (Unit 70)	register your departure
drop off (Unit 53)	leave something/someone at an arranged place
fill in/out (Unit 23, 33)	complete a form
go out of business (Unit 44)	stop doing business
hang up (on) (Unit 37)	put the phone down
look forward to (Unit 30)	wait for/expect with pleasure
look after (Unit 25)	supervise
pick up (Unit 53)	take something/someone from an arranged place
stand for (Unit 18)	mean (initials, abbreviations)
take care of (Unit 10)	be responsible for/deal with
take off (Unit 18)	leave the ground (plane)
	remove (clothing/accessories)
turn on (Unit 16)	start a machine, radio etc.
turn off (Unit 17)	stop a machine, radio etc.
wake up (Unit 21)	stop sleeping

SURVIVAL FILE 14: Prepositions

ABOUT
about 3 months (Unit 10) — Approximate length of time
How about? (Unit 29) — Idiomatic use for suggestion

AHEAD
not three hours ahead (Unit 37) — In front or time zones

AT
at 10:30 (3) / at night (Unit 54) — Time
at gas stations (Unit 1) — Public places
at C.B.W. (Unit 5) — Names of companies
at the Devereux's house (Unit 20) — People's houses
at the sales conference (Unit 45) — Events

BETWEEN ☐●☐
between the man... and the man (Unit 42)

BY
by the day after tomorrow (Unit 55) — Last delay/deadline
by credit card (Unit 32) — Way of doing something

FOR
for 4 nights (Unit 8) — Length of time
F for fox-trot (Unit 30) — As in...
the code for Hollywood (Unit 31) — Belonging to

FROM
from England (Unit 1) — Origin
from our Boston office (Unit 37) — Place you've come from

IN
in January 1961 (Unit 3) — Months, years
in the morning (Unit 37) — Parts of the day
in one hour (Unit 57) — At the end of a period of time
in Atlanta (Unit 1) — Towns, states, countries
in the restaurant (Unit 8) — Public places when inside

IN FRONT OF ☐■
the car in front (of) (Unit 54)

NEXT TO ●☐
sit next to me (Unit 20)

ON
on December 19th (Unit 3) — Dates, days
on the weekend (Unit 61) — Also *at* (U.K.)
on the street (Unit 10) — Streets, roads...
on a Boeing 767 (Unit 18) — Transportation
on business/vacation (Unit 1) — Idiomatic use
on the phone (Unit 30) — Phone, radio, TV

PER
per night (Unit 9) — For each. Also *a*.

TO (INTO, ONTO)
to the Sheraton (Unit 1) — After verbs of movement with destination. Exception: *home*
into Chicago (Unit 30)

UNTIL
until next Sunday (Unit 11) — Up to a certain time

WITH
Enjoy your stay with us (Unit 8) — In the company of
the man with a beard (Unit 42) — Physical features

1. Nouns are divided into two groups: **Uncountable nouns** are things we *can't* count and don't think of as separate. They don't have a plural form. **Countable nouns** are things we *can* count and that have a singular and a plural form.

Uncountable nouns	Countable nouns
traffic	car(s)
change	cent(s)
money	dollar(s)
writing paper	envelope(s)
chewing gum	pack(s) of gum

2. Use **some** and **any** before plural countable nouns and uncountable nouns when amount isn't important. **Not any** and **no** are used for **no quantity.**

Affirmative: use **some**	There is **some** traffic.
	There are **some** cars.
Negative: use **any**	There **isn't any** / is **no** traffic.
	There **aren't any** / are **no** cars.
Questions: use **any**	Is there **any** traffic?
	Are there **any** cars?

3. **A lot of** or **lots of** are used for a large quantity of uncountable or countable nouns.
There is **a lot of** money.　　There are **lots of** dollars.

*TV commercials cost **lots of** money.* (Unit 63)

4. Use expressions of quantity in the following way:

	Uncountable nouns	Countable nouns
small quantity	*A little/not much*	*A few/not many*
question	*How much...?*	*How many...?*
excess quantity	*Too much*	*Too many*

*How **many** pages are there?* (Unit 27)
*I had **a few** questions.* (Unit 67)
*I think I have **too many** charge cards already.* (Unit 53)

5. **More, less** or **fewer** are used to compare quantities.

*There is **more** writing paper.*
*There are **more** envelopes.*
*There is **less** writing paper.*
*There are **fewer** envelopes.*
*...**less** leisure, **less** TV and **more** work.* (Unit 64)

A Adjectives

1. Adjectives go before nouns. When there are two or three adjectives, you usually put them in this order:

	your opinion of the person/thing	size	age	color	origin	
the	funny	little	(old)	(brown-haired)	–	man (Unit 43)
the	attractive	small	–	gray-haired	(American)	woman (Unit 43)

2. Comparatives & Superlatives

Short adjectives	new	new**er (than)**	the new**est**
	big	bigg**er (than)**	the bigg**est**
Short adjectives ending in **y**	easy	eas**ier (than)**	the eas**iest**
Long adjectives	expensive	**more** expensive **(than)**	**the most** expensive
Irregular adjectives	good	**better (than)**	**the best**
	bad	**worse (than)**	**the worst**

*It's **much better than** the one we use at C.B.W.* (Unit 44)
*City and state workers are **the laziest** you'll find.* (Unit 64)

To compare things, we can also say:

Short adjectives	It's not as easy as ...	It's not the easiest
Long adjectives	It's less expensive (than)...	It's the least expensive

*It's probably **less expensive**, too.* (Unit 44)

Adverbs

1. Adverbs go after verbs or at the end of sentences. Usually **ly** is added to an adjective to make an adverb.

    *I don't know him **personally**.* (Unit 41)
    *Advertisers have to choose their medium **carefully**.* (Unit 63)

    Sometimes the adjective is left as it is.
    *You shouldn't drive too **close** to cars in front of you.* (Unit 54)

    There are also some irregular adverbs.
    good — **well**

2. Adverbs of frequency *(always, usually, often, sometimes, seldom, rarely, never)* go before verbs except **be**.

    *In America, you **usually** give tips to waiters.* (Unit 1)
    *He's **never** late.*

    To ask about the frequency of something, use the question **How often?**
    ***How often** do you stay in hotels?* (Unit 59)

3. Note that adverbial phrases such as **very much, very well** and **a lot** go after the object.

    *Wilbur didn't like Copacabana Beach **very much**.* (Unit 49)

Infinitive	Past Simple	Past Participle	Infinitive	Past Simple	Past Participle
be	was	been	hold	held	held
begin	began	begun	keep	kept	kept
break	broke	broken	know	knew	known
bring	brought	brought	leave	left	left
build	built	built	let	let	let
buy	bought	bought	lose	lost	lost
catch	caught	caught	make	made	made
choose	chose	chosen	mean	meant	meant
come	came	come	meet	met	met
cost	cost	cost	pay	paid	paid
cut	cut	cut	put	put	put
deal	dealt	dealt	read	read	read
do	did	done	say	said	said
draw	drew	drawn	see	saw	seen
drink	drank	drunk	sell	sold	sold
drive	drove	driven	send	sent	sent
eat	ate	eaten	set	set	set
fall	fell	fallen	show	showed	shown
feel	felt	felt	shut	shut	shut
find	found	found	sit	sat	sat
fly	flew	flown	speak	spoke	spoken
forbid	forbade	forbidden	spend	spent	spent
forget	forgot	forgotten	stand	stood	stood
get	got	gotten/got	take	took	taken
give	gave	given	teach	taught	taught
go	went	gone	tell	told	told
hang	hung	hung	think	thought	thought
have	had	had	understand	understood	understood
hear	heard	heard	wake	woke	woken
hit	hit	hit	write	wrote	written

Transcript

9 Hotel Information

CONVERSATION A

Man: Studios Inn Hotel. This is Kevin speaking. How may I help you?

Woman: Good afternoon. Do you have any accommodation for tonight?

Man: Yes, ma'am. What are you looking for?

Woman: A room for two adults, and two small kids.

Man: Excuse me … Yes, we have that.

Woman: How much will that be?

Man: The room charge will be $250 per night. The children stay free.

Woman: Great. I'll take it. My name is BERTORELLI. That's B-E…

CONVERSATION C

Front Desk Clerk: What kind of room would you like?

You: I'd like a single room, please.

Front Desk Clerk: Fine. I have a single room available.

You: Does it have a bath?

Front Desk Clerk: No, it doesn't. It has a shower.

You: That's OK.

Front Desk Clerk: How are you paying?

You: With travelers checks.

14 A Deli Sandwich

Nancy Lee: Hi, I'd like a corned beef sandwich, please.

Counter Help: Will that be on white, rye, or whole wheat bread?

Nancy Lee: On Whole wheat, please.

Counter Help: Would you like ketchup, mayonnaise, or mustard?

Nancy Lee: I'd like mustard, please.

Counter Help: Will that be hot or regular?

Nancy Lee: Regular, please.

Counter Help: Would you like lettuce or cabbage on that?

Nancy Lee: Lettuce.

Counter Help: We have romaine, endive, radicchio, or ordinary lettuce.

Nancy Lee: I'd like romaine.

Counter Help: All right. Coming right up!

Nancy Lee: Thank you.

Counter Help: Do you want anything else with that?

Nancy Lee: Ah, I'd like a small coleslaw and a bag of potato chips.

Counter Help: Do you want regular potato chips, chili flavor, blue cheese flavor… ?

Nancy Lee: Regular. And could I have a dill pickle?

Counter Help: Sure. Here you are, ma'am.

Nancy Lee: Great.

Counter Help: That'll be $3.95 altogether.

Nancy Lee: There you go.

Counter Help: Out of five. Thank you very much.

Nancy Lee: Thanks. Oh, I forgot. I want a coffee, too.

Counter Help: OK. We have regular coffee, Colombian special blend, Brazilian, Kenyan, Java, expresso, cappuccino or decaffeinated. The decaffeinated comes in regular, Colombian, or expresso only. You can have that with milk, cream, or low-fat creamer. And we have white sugar, brown sugar, unrefined Barbados sugar, or Sweet 'n Low. We have five sizes. Medium, large, extra large, incredibly large, or you can just take the jumbo king-size…

18 In Flight

ANNOUNCEMENT 1

This is your captain. My name is Roy Conway, and I'd like to thank you for choosing United Airlines. Welcome aboard our Boeing 767, flight 755 to Denver. We're just waiting for clearance from Air Traffic Control, and then we'll be on our way. I'd like to remind you to keep your seat belts fastened, and also that smoking is not permitted on flights of less than four hours duration.

ANNOUNCEMENT 2

This is your Captain speaking, again. Sorry folks, I'm afraid we have an air traffic delay. It'll be 30 minutes before we can take off. So sit back, relax and our flight attendants will serve you drinks courtesy of United Airlines. We'd like to apologize for this delay, but, at this time, it's beyond our control.

ANNOUNCEMENT 3

Hi, folks. We're now cruising at 30,000 feet and I've just turned off the "Fasten Seat Belts" sign. I would like to remind you that for your comfort, safety and convenience, you should keep your seat belts fastened at all times. I'm hoping to make up some of the lost time, and I'll be reporting on our progress later in the flight. Our flight attendants will be serving lunch in a moment. Thank you.

ANNOUNCEMENT 4

This is Roy Conway, your captain speaking. I have some good news. We have made up some lost time, and our E.T.A. (that's estimated time of arrival) in Denver, is now 7:45 p.m. Mountain Time. If you want to set your watches, it is now 7:21 Mountain Time, and we'll soon be commencing with our descent into Denver. The temperature on the ground is 29° Fahrenheit, with clear skies and some light snow cover. I hope you all remembered to pack your winter coats. It's mighty cold down there.

ANNOUNCEMENT 5

We're now taxiing in to our gate. May I remind you to remain in your seats with your seat belts fastened until the aircraft has come to a complete standstill. It is now 7:52. Passengers with connecting flights should report *immediately* to the Transfer Desk in Concourse A. Thank you for flying United Airlines and we hope you'll fly with us again soon.

19 Congratulations!

Wilbur Meeks walked into the Chief Executive's office and sat down. "Good going, Meeks - a tremendous job!" said Mr. Devereux, the Chief Executive. "Sit down. Have a cigar!"

"I don't smoke, sir."

The Chief Executive closed the cigar box. "Now, you're British, aren't you?" asked Mr. Devereux.

"That's right sir, but my wife's American."

"And how long have you been with us?" asked Mr. Devereux.

"Only three weeks, sir, but I came from the Boston office."

"Well, I just wanted to say, congratulations!"

"Thank you, sir," said Wilbur with a smile. Then he thought for a moment. "Um … I don't understand, sir," he said.

"Congratulations – you've done very well," the Chief Executive repeated.

Wilbur looked surprised. "I don't know what you mean," he said.

The Chief Executive smiled. "The new contract – the one you got from Burlingham Inc? I'm very happy about it. In fact, I want you to come over to my house for dinner on Sunday. How about that?"

Wilbur Meeks looked at the floor. "Well, it's not *that* good," he said.

"Good! It's great – a five hundred thousand dollar contract is good work, Meeks … ah, William."

"My name's not William, sir. It's *Wilbur.*"

"Didn't I say 'Wilbur'?" said the Chief Executive.

"No, sorry, sir. You didn't. Excuse me, but did you just say five hundred thousand? May I see my letter?" said Wilbur.

The Chief Executive passed it to him. "Here you are, Wilbur, my friend," he said with a smile.

"I'm afraid there's a mistake, sir," said Wilbur. "There are too many zeros – well, actually there's a period missing. I meant five *thousand dollars and no cents.* Um, what time should I come for dinner on Sunday, sir?"

22 A Trip To The Mall

CONVERSATION 1

Salesclerk: Can I help you?

Consuela: Yes, I was looking at that sweater in the window.

Salesclerk: The pink and gray one?

Consuela: No, the blue one.

Salesclerk: Oh! The man's sweater.

Consuela: That's right. It's for my husband. What colors does it come in?

Salesclerk: We have navy blue, dark green and pale blue.

Consuela: Hmm. Do you have a navy blue one in an Extra Large?

Salesclerk: Let's see … small, medium, large … oh yes, here you are. Extra Large. It's a good quality sweater. 100% wool, made in Italy.

Consuela: Sure. I'll take it. How much is that?

Salesclerk: Forty-nine dollars and ninety-five cents.

CONVERSATION 2

Salesclerk: Hello, there. May I help you?

Consuela: Hello. Yes, I guess so. I'm looking for a toy, for an eight-year-old boy.

Salesclerk: Does he have a video games console?

Consuela: Yes, he does.

Salesclerk: We have some new games in. This is Mega Mario Five. It's very popular.

Consuela: OK. How much is it?

Salesclerk: Twenty-nine, ninety-nine.

CONVERSATION 3

Consuela: I'll take these, please.

Salesclerk: OK. Size eight, right?

Consuela: That's right.

Salesclerk: They're just in. We got them yesterday.

Consuela: Oh, great. They're my size. Thirty-nine, fifty, isn't it?

Salesclerk: Yeah. Out of fifty. That's ten fifty change. They're excellent jeans. I think I'm gonna buy a pair for myself.

CONVERSATION 4

Consuela: Pardon me, do you have any Nike Air?

Salesclerk: Right over there, ma'am. The Nike display is between the Reeboks and the L.A. Gear.

Consuela: Oh, yes. I didn't see them there. Do you have a pair of these in size three and a half?

Salesclerk: I think so. Yes, we do. Do you want to try them on?

Consuela: What? Oh, no! They're way too small for me. They're for my daughter.

Salesclerk: Ooops! Sorry... They're eighty-nine, forty-five.

Consuela: OK. Do you take credit cards?

23 At the Post Office

Consuela Rodriguez: Good morning. I'd like to send this package to Mexico.

Clerk: I'll need you to fill in a customs form, please.

Consuela Rodriguez: Sure. Business papers - no, Contents in detail, um, sweater. Yes, it's a gift. Value - um, fifty dollars … weight - oh, I don't know the weight.

Clerk: Put it on the scale.

Consuela Rodriguez: There you go.

Clerk: OK, that's one pound, two ounces.

Consuela Rodriguez: Really? How much is that in kilograms?

Clerk: Oh, about half a kilo. Now is this surface mail or air mail?

Consuela Rodriguez: Air mail, please.

Clerk: That's going to be $13.72.

Consuela Rodriguez: Thank you.

Clerk: Out of twenty. That's five … six dollars and twenty-eight cents change.

Consuela Rodriguez: When do you think it'll get to Mexico?

Clerk: There's no guarantee, ma'am, but I guess the day after tomorrow.

Consuela Rodriguez: Thanks.

30 On the Phone

Jessica Adams: Hello.

Linda Foster: Is this Jessica Adams?

Jessica Adams: Speaking.

Linda Foster: Hi, this is Linda Foster.

Jessica Adams: What?

Linda Foster: I said, "this is Linda Foster".

Jessica Adams: Who?

Linda Foster: Linda Foster. Can't you hear me?

Jessica Adams: Not very well. It's a bad line.

Linda Foster: Linda Foster. That's F for fox-trot, O for Oscar, S for Sierra, T for tango, E for echo, R for Romeo.

Jessica Adams: Oh, Foster! Linda Foster from Devereux Computers.

Linda Foster: That's right. I'm flying into Chicago from Seattle tomorrow. Could you meet me at the Standard Club at ten-thirty?

Jessica Adams: Yeah, sure, Linda. Ten-thirty at the Standard Club. I'll look forward to seeing you.

Linda Foster: OK, I'll see you tomorrow. Bye.

Jessica Adams: Bye.

31 Telephone facilities

QUESTION 2

Recorded message: Thank you for calling the Studios Inn Hotel. If you are calling from a touch-tone phone, you can select the department you want *now* or at any time during this call. If you want to enquire about reservations, press 'two' *now*. If you want to speak to hotel management, press 'eight' *now*. If you want to speak to the Guest Services, press 'four' *now*. If you want to enquire about conference facilities and reservations, press 'nine' *now*. If you want Business Services, press 'six' *now*. If you wish to speak to a guest, and you know the room number that you require, press 'one' followed by the room number *now*. If you require further assistance please hold for the operator.

Operator: Studios Inn Hotel. This is the operator. How can I help you?

33 Lost Baggage

CONVERSATION C

Wilbur: Devereux Computers, Boston office?

Airline Representative: May I speak to Mr. Meeks?

Wilbur: This is he.

Airline Representative: This is Redwood Airlines. You lost your suitcase three days ago? We have some news for you.

Wilbur: Great!

Airline Representative: First the good news. We've found your suitcase. Now the bad news. It isn't in Boston.

Wilbur: Where is it?

Airline Representative: Well, it went from Seattle on the flight to Bangkok. Then it went to Hong Kong. They put it on the flight to New York, but it didn't get there. They took it off the plane in L.A. Then it went to Seattle.

Wibur: That's OK. Can you send it to my home address?

Airline Representative: Ah, no. They then sent it to Bologna, in Italy!

34 Airport Arrivals

Immigration Inspector: Good morning. Where have you come from?

Tadashi Nakamura: Tokyo, Japan.

Immigration Inspector: Fine. May I see your passport?

Tadashi Nakamura: Here you are.

Immigration Inspector: What's the nature of your visit?

Tadashi Nakamura: Business. I'm visiting my company's West Coast office.

Immigration Inspector: And how long are you staying in the United States?

Tadashi Nakamura: About three weeks.

Immigration Inspector: Fine. Here's your passport back.

Tadashi Nakamura: Thank you.

Immigration Inspector: Welcome to the United States. Enjoy your stay.

35 Customs

QUESTION 1

Customs Officer: Excuse me. Do you have anything to declare?

Natalie Trudeau: Well, I have some whiskey.

Customs Officer: How much whiskey do you have?

Natalie Trudeau: One bottle. It's a liter, I think.

Customs Officer: That's OK. Do you have anything else?

Natalie Trudeau: Yes, I have some perfume.

Customs Officer: There are no restrictions on perfume for personal use. Is that all?

Natalie Trudeau: Yes, that's it.

Customs Officer: That's OK. You can go through.

36 Asking for Directions

QUESTION 3

CONVERSATION A

1st Man: Pardon me, I'm trying to get to the Walk of Fame.

2nd Man: I can't help you. I don't know the area.

1st Man: OK. Thanks anyway.

1st Man: Excuse me, I'm trying to get to the Walk of Fame. Can you give me directions?

3rd Man: Pardon me?

1st Man: Do you know how to get to the Walk of Fame?

3rd Man: Ain't that where they have all the footprints of the stars in the sidewalk?

1st Man: Yes, that's it.

3rd Man: I've seen that on TV. I reckon it's round here somewhere.

1st Man: But you don't know where?

3rd Man: Nope, sorry. Can't help ya.

1st Man: Excuse me, can you give me directions to the Walk of Fame?

1st Woman: Are you driving or walking?

1st Man: Driving.

1st Woman: It's the same anyhow. You just hang a left onto Highland, right?

1st Man: I go right onto Highland?

1st Woman: No, you turn left onto Highland. Right … sorry, I mean… OK. Then take the first right onto Hollywood Boulevard. It's about half a mile down, maybe a bit less. You'll see it on your left, just before the next intersection. That's the northeast corner of Hollywood and Vine.

CONVERSATION B

2nd Woman: Excuse me but, can you give me directions to Union Station, from here?

3rd Woman: That's pretty far from here. What you gotta do is stay on Sunset until you see the sign for the I-101. Then get off of Sunset and take that freeway. About four or five miles down on the 101, you'll start to see the signs for the station, but I don't remember the exit number. Anyhow, you want the exit for the I-110 North. Then start looking for the exit to Sunset Blvd. Take that until you hit Olvera Street. You'll see the signs for the station before then. Can't miss 'em.

2nd Woman: Couldn't I just stay on Sunset the whole way?

3rd Woman: Yeah, but it'll be a lot quicker on the Freeway at this time of day.

2nd Woman: Right. Thanks.

CONVERSATION C

4th Man: Hi, guys. Which way to Paramount Pictures?

1st Kid: Did you say Paramount Pictures?

4th Man: That's right.

2nd Kid: Well, go straight at this intersection and then take a right at the next intersection onto Vine. Go past Santa Monica Boulevard and get ready to go left onto Melrose. It's right along there. There's a huge bill board outside the entrance.

4th Man: Thanks, guys.

2nd Kid: You're welcome.

1st Kid: Hey, haven't I seen you before on TV?

4th Man: Yeah. I guess so.

2nd Kid: Hey! It's Michael Jackson! Wow, look everyone, it's Michael Jackson!

38 A Job Interview

CONVERSATION A

Ms. Dukakis: Come in. Mr. Lo, isn't it? Please have a seat.

Mr. Lo: Thank you.

Ms. Dukakis: Did you have a good trip?

Mr. Lo: Yes, thanks. I came up from San Diego yesterday.

Ms. Dukakis: And did you find a nice hotel?

Mr. Lo: No. I'm staying at my parent's place in Oakland.

Ms. Dukakis: Oh, that's right, you're from the Bay area, aren't you?

Mr. Lo: Yes. I was born and raised in Oakland.

Ms. Dukakis: When did you leave?

Mr. Lo: I went to college in L.A. That was in 1988.

Ms. Dukakis: So, where are you presently working?

Mr. Lo: Soledad Computers in San Diego. Have you heard of them?

Ms. Dukakis: No, not really. How long have you been with them?

Mr. Lo: I've been working there since I graduated from college.

Ms. Dukakis: Why do you want to change jobs now?

Mr. Lo: I'd like to do some traveling. I want to use my languages, and I want a better job.

Ms. Dukakis: Yes. I see here that you speak Chinese and Spanish. ¿Puede usted traducírmelo?

Mr. Lo: Pardon me? Can you say that more slowly?

Ms. Dukakis: That's OK. Do you want to live closer to your parents?

Mr. Lo: That's not the reason why I want this job. But yes, I'd like to live in this area again.

Ms. Dukakis: Well, thank you, Mr. Lo. We'll be in touch.

CONVERSATION B

Ms. Dukakis: Come in, Ms. Danziger. Please have a …

Ms. Danziger: Please call me Crystal. My, you have a nice office.

Ms. Dukakis: Thank you. Did you have a good trip?

Ms. Danziger: It was OK. I got in on the early flight this morning.

Ms. Dukakis: Ah, you're from Los Angeles, aren't you?

Ms. Danziger: I live in L.A at the present time, but I'm originally from New York. Of course, I'm not often in L.A. I've been to seven countries this year.

Ms. Dukakis: Tell me about your present job.

Ms. Danziger: I'm a sales representative for a book publisher … Travel Books Incorporated. We sell guide books and maps. I travel around Latin America. You see from my resume that I speak Spanish and Portuguese. I majored in Spanish for my Bachelors degree and then …

Ms. Dukakis: Where did you get your degree?

Ms. Danziger: I got it from the University of Chicago. Then, after that, I did my Masters at the University of New Mexico.

Ms. Dukakis: How long have you been with Travel Books?

Ms. Danziger: Two years. Before that I was with the Disney company for a year in Florida, and before that I worked at a commercial stationery company in Dallas for six months.

Ms. Dukakis: Have you ever sold computer software?

Ms. Danziger: No, but selling is selling. It's all the same to me.

Ms. Dukakis: And do you speak any Asian languages?

Ms. Danziger: No, but I learn fast. I majored in languages. Now, *I* want to ask *you* some questions about this job …

40 Breakfast in America

Waitress: Hi! <u>How are you doing?</u> Are you ready to order?

Ian King: Yes, I am, thank you. <u>I'll have</u> the Farmer's Breakfast.

Waitress: <u>How would you like</u> your eggs - sunnyside-up, over-easy or …?

Ian King: Sunnyside-up.

Waitress: Oh, I see. You're British! Well, that's when the egg's not flipped over. You can also have your eggs poached or scrambled.

Ian King: Uh, <u>I think I'll have them</u> sunnyside-up.

Waitress: <u>And will that be</u> link sausage, bacon, or country ham?

Ian King: <u>Bacon</u>, please. Instead of the grits, <u>could I have</u> pancakes?

Waitress: Sorry, sir. I'm afraid the pancakes <u>will</u> be a side order.

Ian King: All right, then. <u>A side order</u> of pancakes.

Waitress: Anything to drink?

Ian King: <u>Ah, yes.</u> A coffee, please, and freshly-squeezed orange juice.

Waitress: Cream and sugar are <u>on the table</u>. I'll bring your coffee <u>and juice </u>right away.

Ian King: <u>Thank you. Could I also have</u> a glass of water?

Waitress: Sure. Coming right up.

46 A Software Brochure

1

Wilbur Meeks: What do you mean, Miss Hawkins? I think every company needs a Draw program. Yes, I know you're a lawyer. Well, yes, I agree that a lawyer's letters need to look serious. What about the logo on your letterhead? Oh, it's in silver and blue. Well, yes, I agree. You can't print that on a laserwriter. Well, drawing is fun - you can draw pictures when you're not busy. Oh, I see. You're always busy. Anyway, take it home. The kids will love it. Oh, yes. Sorry. You don't have any kids. So, you really don't want any drawing software, then?

2

Wilbur Meeks: This is really selling well. Our Boston office alone sold nearly two thousand copies last month. Most of the buyers are small business people with just one or two computers. It's probably the only program they will have. The word processor is pretty basic, but it's fine for letters and mail-merging and that kind of thing. A small business can use the spreadsheet for accounting. They won't need a dedicated accounting package. I think you could use a lot of these. Can I write you down for 2000 copies? No? Right. Just the one, then.

3

Wilbur Meeks: It's great. I'm terrible at spelling and grammar, but it corrects everything for me. You can record notes on the text through a microphone. You know, if you're writing a letter you can add notes for yourself.

Mr. Bland: I don't really understand.

Wilbur Meeks: Let me demonstrate, Mr. Bland. Um … this is a copy of the letter I sent to you, when I arranged the meeting. You see that little black picture of a microphone? Just there, in the middle of the screen. I just click on that once with the mouse, and I get a voice message. Listen.

Computerized voice: Remember. Go very slowly with old Mr. Bland. He knows nothing about computers. In fact, he's a complete fool. He'll buy anything!

Wilbur Meeks: Oh! I forgot I recorded that earlier … I really am very sorry …

49 Describing Places

Max Devereux: We mixed business with pleasure, really. I had to go to Japan for business and Helena came with me. We went down to Kyoto after I finished doing business in Tokyo. It was October, and the fall is really beautiful in Kyoto. It's like New England or parts of Canada, just fantastic fall colors, and clean crisp air out of the city. Of course, we got a little rain, but it didn't matter. We stayed in a traditional Japanese hotel, a Ryokan. The temples are beautiful. It wasn't as quiet as I would like. There were lots of schoolkids at all of the temples. But they're magic places. Just magic. You have to see all of the temples, but my favorite was The Golden Pavilion.

Natalie Trudeau: Vacation? I always take my main vacation in the middle of winter. I've been to Switzerland once before. I love to ski. The scenery is amazing, the mountains are spectacular. Yes, I go to St Moritz. I suppose most of the people who go there are pretty rich … sometimes even European royalty. And it really is an action-packed vacation. You don't go up there to relax. There are great… but expensive… restaurants to go to in the evening, and some fantastic designer jewelry and clothing stores. Yeah, I like it. I'll go again this year.

Charlene Meeks: Wilbur and I went on a cruise for our honeymoon. It was a shame that Wilbur was so sea-sick, but we had a good time … when he wasn't feeling sick, that is. The place I remember best is Rio de Janeiro. We arrived there right in the middle of Mardi Gras! Everyone is in the streets, and there's tons of noise and excitement! Wilbur got lost of course, but the police found him and brought him back to the ship. Oh, yes, and Copacabana Beach. Wilbur didn't like that very much. He got so badly sunburned. Wow, was his face red! It's the hole in the ozone layer, he figures.

50 Reserving an Airline Ticket

Travel Agent: Good morning. Can I help you?

Nancy Lee: <u>Yes, I'd like to reserve a seat for a flight to Hong-Kong.</u>

Travel Agent: Hong Kong? Would that be a round-trip ticket or one-way?

Nancy Lee: <u>Round-trip, please.</u>

Travel Agent: And for what date?

Nancy Lee: <u>The eighteenth, if possible.</u>

Travel Agent: Friday, the eighteenth? Yes. That's fine. What about the return date? Do you have a fixed date in mind, or do you want an open ticket?

Nancy Lee: <u>An open ticket.</u>

Travel Agent: OK. Do you want a morning flight, or an afternoon flight?

Nancy Lee: <u>What's available?</u>

Travel Agent: Well, there's a Cathay Pacific flight at ten-thirty and a US Air one at twelve-thirty.

Nancy Lee: <u>I'll take the Cathay Pacific one.</u>

Travel Agent: OK. If you'll just hold on a minute, I'll check to see if there's room. Yes, that's fine.

Nancy Lee: <u>Oh, good. How much is it?</u>

Travel Agent: One thousand, eight hundred and seventy dollars.

Nancy Lee: <u>OK. Thanks.</u>

Travel Agent: Now, can I have your details, please?

51 Reservations

CONVERSATION B

Announcement: Thank you for calling the Hudson Theater. All our lines are busy at this time. Please hold. Thank you for calling the Hud…

Michael Robertson: Oh, no! Darn!

Ticket Sales: Pardon me? This is the Hudson Theater Box Office. Jasmine speaking.

Michael Robertson: Oh, sorry. Do you have four tickets for "Carmen" on Thursday night?

Ticket Sales: We have very few tickets left for that performance. Where would you like to sit?

Michael Robertson: In the center, close to the stage?

Ticket Sales: Those seats were sold out months ago, sir. However, we have seats available in the lower and upper balconies.

Michael Robertson: Well, the lower balcony.

Ticket Sales: Do you all want to sit together?

Michael Robertson: Uh? Yes!

Ticket Sales: I don't have four seats together in the lower balcony. I have two and two.

Michael Robertson: No, I want four together. The upper balcony, then.

Ticket Sales: Fine. I have ZZ54, 55, 56 and 57. Should I mail them, or do you want to pick them up on the night?

Michael Robertson: I'll pick them up.

Ticket Sales: Then you have to be here one hour before the performance, unless you want to pay now. In which case, you can pick them up as late as you like.

Michael Robertson: I'll pay now.

Ticket Sales: Which card?

Michael Robertson: MasterCard.

Ticket Sales: Number?

Michael Robertson: Five, four, one, two. Three, four, five, six. Seven, eight, nine, zero. One, two, three four.

Ticket Sales: Expiration date?

Michael Robertson: Zero, eight, two thousand.

Ticket Sales: The name as printed on the card?

Michael Robertson: Mr. Michael Robertson.

Ticket Sales: I'll read that back. Mastercard. Five, four, one, two. Three, four, five, six. Seven, nine, zero. One, two, three, four. Expiration date eight, two thousand. In the name of Mr. Michael Robertson. Four seats in the upper balcony.

Michael Robertson: That's correct.

Ticket Sales: The total cost will be one hundred and forty dollars.

Michael Robertson: That's fine. Thank you.

53   Renting a Car

Natalie Trudeau: Good morning. I'd like <u>to rent a car</u>, please.

Clerk: Yes, ma'am. For <u>how long</u>?

Natalie Trudeau: For three days.

Clerk: All right. Where <u>do you want</u> to leave the car?

Natalie Trudeau: <u>Can I</u> leave it at the downtown office?

Clerk: Sure – you can <u>leave</u> our cars at any of our offices. What kind of car <u>do you want</u>?

Natalie Trudeau: <u>Can I see</u> your brochure?

Clerk: <u>There you go.</u>

Natalie Trudeau: Uh, it's not important really. <u>How about</u> this one?

Clerk: OK. <u>May I see your</u> driver's license?

Natalie Trudeau: I have an International Driver's License and a French one.

Clerk: Fine. Thank you. Now, <u>do you want</u> C.D.W and personal accident insurance?

Natalie Trudeau: Sure. I'll take both.

Clerk: Right, can you check these two boxes, and put your initials here, and again here.

Natalie Trudeau: <u>There you go.</u>

Clerk: How do you want <u>to pay</u>?

Natalie Trudeau: American Express, please.

Clerk: That's fine. Would you be interested in our Federal Charge Card? It can be used at any Federal Rental Office.

Natalie Trudeau: I think I have too <u>many</u> charge cards already.

55   Communications

Nathan: Good afternoon, Mr. Thomas. You wanted to see me.

Ryan: Oh, Nathan. Come in.

Nathan: Thanks.

Ryan: I have some mail. Can you take care of it for me?

Nathan: Sure. How do you want it sent?

Ryan: OK. This is the most urgent. Can you fax it through to Consuela Rodriguez? I think it's better to send it to the hotel in San Francisco. She's seeing a client there today, and won't be back in L.A. until tomorrow.

Nathan: OK. Should I send a hard copy by mail to confirm?

Ryan: There's no need. She's leaving the hotel tomorrow anyway. This is the contract with Consuela's company. They need it in Mexico City, as soon as possible. Can you call the courier service and ask them to pick it up?

Nathan: Sure. We may be too late for the evening flight.

Ryan: That's OK. If it goes on the early flight tomorrow morning, they'll get it in the afternoon. That's fine. The New York office needs a copy of the German contract. I want our lawyers to check it out and make a few changes. I haven't printed it out. Just download it to their E-Mail number.

Nathan: I'll do it right away.

Ryan: Not so fast, Nathan. The phone call's cheaper after six o'clock. There's nobody at the New York office now anyway. It's 8 p.m. Then send this floppy disk to Taipei. It's not real urgent, but send it Express anyway. That way someone has to sign for it. The letter to Frankfurt can go standard airmail. The same for the postcard. Oh, and our distributor in Osaka has asked for one hundred catalogs. They can go surface mail. There's no hurry.

Nathan: OK. Good night, Mr. Thomas.

Ryan: Good night Nathan, and thanks a lot.

62   Agreeing and Disagreeing

CONVERSATION A

Wilbur Meeks: Would you like a whiskey, sir?

Mr. Devereux: No, thanks – I <u>don't like</u> whiskey.

Wilbur Meeks: Oh, neither do I, sir. How about a cigarette?

Mr. Devereux: No, thanks – I <u>don't</u> smoke anymore.

Wilbur Meeks: Oh, <u>neither do I</u>, sir. Nasty habit.

Mr. Devereux: Hmm, I <u>like</u> these sandwiches.

Wilbur Meeks: Oh, so do I, sir!

CONVERSATION B

Mr. Devereux: The thing is, our new word processor needs more advertising.

Wilbur Meeks: <u>Exactly.</u>

Mr. Devereux: The question is, what kind of advertising? Now, I've thought a lot about this, and I think we should try a television campaign.

Wilbur Meeks: <u>I couldn't agree more, sir.</u>

Mr. Devereux: A good TV campaign could increase sales by 50 percent.

Wilbur Meeks: <u>Absolutely. You're a genius, sir!</u>

Mr. Devereux: I'm glad you agree, Wilbur. What about you, Linda?

Linda Foster: I'm afraid I don't agree, sir.

Mr. Devereux: What do you mean?

Linda Foster: In my opinion, it's a complete waste of money.

Wilbur Meeks: <u>Oh, I really don't agree</u> - think of all the people who are going to see it.

Linda Foster: They might see it, but will they buy it?

Wilbur Meeks: Yes, I'm sure they will.

Linda Foster: I don't know. Think about it. We're talking about a $630 word processor, not a $29 Nintendo game! This is a serious business tool. We should advertise in the specialist business press!

65   Registering at a Convention

QUESTION 1

CONVERSATION A

Michael Robertson: I wanted to register. Is this the right desk?

Sophie: Which category are you in?

Michael Robertson: I'm just attending the conference.

Sophie: Right. That's here. Category, participant. Great. Did you pre-register?

Michael Robertson: Yes, a couple of months ago. The name's Robertson, initial M.

Sophie: Hold on. Is that M for Michael or M for Marvin?

Michael Robertson: Michael.

Sophie: There's a Marvin Robertson from Columbus, Ohio attending too. Ah, I have your envelope. You're from C.B.W. in Toronto, right?

Michael Robertson: Right.

Sophie: Here's your i.d. pass. The envelope contains your convention planner, a plan of the convention center and the conference handbook.

Michael Robertson: Thank you.

CONVERSATION B

Security Guard: Pardon me, sir. May I see your i.d. pass?

Wilbur Meeks: Pass? What pass! I'm Wilbur Meeks.

Security Guard: Yes, sir. But whoever you are, I still need to see your convention pass. I'm sorry, but you can't go into the convention center without a pass. Are you a participant at the convention?

Wilbur Meeks: Well, I'm not an engineer. I'm an exhibitor. I'm with Devereux Computers. We have a stand in the exhibition hall. I'm sure it's OK.

Security Guard: Well, you need an exhibitor's pass. Participants have blue passes. Exhibitors have pink passes. Would you please report to the desk over there for convention registration?

Wilbur Meeks: Oh, right. OK.

CONVERSATION C

João Santos: Good morning. I'm a speaker at the convention today.

Sophie: OK, sir. Speakers' registration is at the last desk.

João Santos: Thank you.

João Santos: Good morning. I'm a speaker at the convention.

Secretary: Good morning. May I have your name, please?

João Santos: Yes. João Santos. That's J-O-Ã-O, S-A-N-T-O-S. From the Federal University of Brasilia.

Secretary: Ah, yes. Dr. Santos. You're making one of the keynote speeches, right?

João Santos: That's right.

Secretary: We have a yellow pass for speakers. There you go. This envelope contains all the information you need. And here's an invitation to the reception for speakers this evening. It's in the Paramount Suite just off the main lobby.

João Santos: Thank you.

Secretary: Thank you, Dr. Santos.

66   Making Plans

Dr. Santos: Excuse me, <u>can you tell me</u> where the Convention Secretary's office is?

Sophie: Sure. Go down the hall, turn right, and it's the first door on your left.

Dr. Santos: Thank you. Now – what did she say? <u>Turn right and</u> I'll find his door <u>on the left.</u> Oh, here it is. James McGovern – Convention Secretary.

James McGovern: Come in!

Dr. Santos: Good morning. <u>I'm</u> Dr. João Santos.

James McGovern: Well, Dr. Santos, it's a pleasure to <u>meet you.</u>

Dr. Santos: I understand you <u>want</u> me to <u>make</u> a speech tonight.

James McGovern: Yes, <u>I think you're</u> the best person to do it.

Dr. Santos: You <u>want</u> me to <u>welcome</u> the Japanese Ambassador.

James McGovern: That's right.

Dr. Santos: And how long do you want me to speak for?

James McGovern: Oh, about ten or fifteen minutes. You just give him a warm welcome in the name of the engineering profession, and perhaps say a few words about the purpose of the convention.

Dr. Santos: Sure, I can do that.

James McGovern: That's great. I'll leave it to you, then.

Dr. Santos: All right. I'll go and prepare my speech.

James McGovern: Fine. I'll see you at dinner.

Dr. Santos: OK. See you later.

67 Preparing a Speech

Dr. Santos: Come in!

Linda Perez: Dr. Santos? My name's Linda Perez, James McGovern's secretary. I'm typing up your speech from the micro-cassette, and I had a few questions.

Dr. Santos: Oh, come in, Ms. Perez - ah, may I call you Linda?

Linda Perez: Of course, Doctor.

Dr. Santos: Yes, well now, what are the questions?

Linda Perez: How about I play through your tape and stop it where I have a question?

Dr. Santos: All right.

Tape (of Dr. Santos): Your Excellency, Mr. Chairman, Gentlemen –

Linda Perez: Yes, this is the first one. I believe there will be several women present.

Dr. Santos: Women? Oh, yes - then change it to Ladies and Gentlemen.

Linda Perez: All right.

Tape: I have great pleasure in speaking today on behalf of our association –

Linda Perez: Ah, yes. This is the next one. Um, there are two associations represented at the convention, aren't there?

Dr. Santos: Oh, yes, I'd forgotten about the North American Hydraulic Engineering guys. We'd better change that to "our associations".

Linda Perez: All right, Dr. Santos.

Tape: and we are honored today by the presence of His Excellency, the Ambassador of Japan, who has traveled over 5000 miles especially to be present at this, the Sixth International Convention of Civil Engineers.

Linda Perez: Here we are. Um, I think it's less than 3000 miles from Washington D.C. to L.A.

Dr. Santos: Oh, right! I originally put kilometers. Thank you. Change it to "who has traveled nearly 3000 miles especially to be present at this, the Sixth International Convention of Civil Engineers". How does the speech sound to you, Linda?

Linda Perez: Very good, Dr. Santos. I'm sure everyone will be very interested.

68 Convention Planner

Jessica Adams: Hi! Michael! Good to see you.

Michael Robertson: It's good to see you too, Jessica. I enjoyed your presentation.

Jessica Adams: Thank you. Did you have an interesting day?

Michael Robertson: Yes, very interesting.

Jessica Adams: What did you go to?

Michael Robertson: Well, Dr. Santos, of course, and Angela Garcia. She's a lawyer in Toronto, you know. She's done some work for C.B.W.

Jessica Adams: Yes, I've met her. I attended Tadashi Nakamura's seminar after lunch. There are some very interesting developments going on in Japan.

Michael Robertson: Chicago Associated isn't getting interested in underwater systems, are they?

Jessica Adams: No, not at all. I just wanted to find out more about them, that's all.

Michael Robertson: I'm sorry I missed that. I was at Manuel Garcia's seminar. To be honest, it was a bit advanced for me.

Jessica Adams: Yes. Did you see Dr. Santos again in the afternoon?

Michael Robertson: I wanted to, but I already saw the keynote. I thought it was better to see someone else. There was a British guy who's doing some work in Georgia and Florida. I don't remember his name. Good talk, though.

Jessica Adams: Did you speak to Max Devereux yet?

Michael Robertson: Yes, briefly. And I'm pleased to say we're going to have lunch together tomorrow.

Jessica Adams: Great. Well, good luck!

69 Room Service

Consuela: Press eight … right.

Room Service: This is room service. Bart speaking.

Consuela Rodriguez: Good evening. This is room 743. I wanted to order something to eat.

Room Service: Right. Excuse me. Ms. Rodriguez?

Consuela Rodriguez: That's right.

Room Service: What can I do for you?

Consuela Rodriguez: OK. I'll have a Chef's Salad, please.

Room Service: Will that be with Thousand Is …

Consuela Rodriguez: Just oil and vinegar, please.

Room Service: Anything else?

Consuela Rodriguez: Mmm. I'd like some bread.

Room Service: Bread rolls, bread sticks and ice water are included in the price, Ms. Rodriguez.

Consuela Rodriguez: OK, fine. And a glass of dry white wine, please.

Room Service: There are two small bottles of white wine in the mini-bar, Ms. Rodriguez.

Consuela Rodriguez: I know, but I don't care for the brand. I'll take a glass of the California Chardonnay, please.

Room Service: OK.

Consuela Rodriguez: How long will it be?

Room Service: We're not that busy right now. It'll be with you in about twenty minutes.

Consuela Rodriguez: That's great. Now, do I have time to take a shower?

70 Check-out

Max Devereux: OK, Wilbur, can you explain this - and it better be good!

Wilbur Meeks: I'm so sorry, sir. But it's really not my fault. Take the movies – I heard that it was a good idea to leave the TV on in your room, so that thieves wouldn't know the room was empty. I didn't realize I selected the movie rental channel. It was on all day. And then there's the telephone. I had to call a long distance recorded information line, and I guess I didn't put the phone back properly. And the mini-bar was all a mistake! I had this big birthday cake – it's for you, sir – and I wanted to keep it cold, so I took everything out of the mini-bar. I didn't realize that it automatically registered a charge when you removed something. Sir – it's a beautiful cake, really. Well, it was. It got a bit hot overnight and the chocolate melted all over the carpet – um, and the hotel says they're going to charge me for cleaning the carpet, sir. Can I put that on my room account? Anyway, the only other thing was breakfast. I went to a table, and there were five people sitting there. When the waiter came and asked for our room numbers, they all said they were with me – I thought they were just being friendly. What I didn't realize was that I was paying for their breakfasts. I'm really, really sorry.

72 Good-Bye

CONVERSATION A

Consuela Rodriguez: Well, good-bye, Ryan. Don't forget, if you're ever in Mexico City, you should come and see us.

Ryan Thomas: I will. And we'll see you again next year?

Consuela Rodriguez: Of course.

Ryan Thomas: I hope the hotel was OK.

Consuela Rodriguez: Oh, yes. It was fine. Except for the last few days. It's been full of people for the Engineer's Convention!

CONVERSATION B

Max Devereux: So, I'll look forward to seeing you in Seattle.

Michael Robertson: Yes. I'll report back to my bosses in Toronto tomorrow, and I'll call your secretary to arrange a meeting.

Max Devereux: I certainly think we can do business together, Michael.

Michael Robertson: I hope so.

CONVERSATION C

Bell Captain: Excuse me! Mr. Meeks!

Wilbur Meeks: Ah, yes?

Bell Captain: The Front Desk Manager wanted to speak to you before you leave, sir.

Wilbur Meeks: I'm in a hurry. I have a plane to catch.

Bell Captain: It will only take a moment, sir. There's something about a cleaning charge for your carpet …

CONVERSATION D

James McGovern: Thank you again, Dr. Santos. It's been a pleasure having you here. And thank you for your impressive speech!

João Santos: Well, thank you for all your help.

James McGovern: That's what I'm here for.

João Santos: Well, it's been nice to meet you. Good-bye.

Wordlist

ENGLISH	FRENCH	JAPANESE	GERMAN
acceptance 41	acceptation	承諾	Akzeptierung
accident 54	accident	事故	Unfall
account 27, 70	note	勘定書	Konto
address 33, 34, 38, 47, 56	adresse	住所	Adresse
adult 52	adulte	大人	Erwachsene/r
advertiser 63	annonceur	広告主	Inserent/in
advertising 62, 63	publicité	広告	Werbung
agreement 64	accord	協定	Übereinkunft
air conditioned 52	climatisé	エアコン付きの	klimatisiert
air conditioning 58, 59	climatisation	冷暖房	Klimaanlage
airmail 55	par avion	航空便	Luftpost
airport 2, 16, 18, 25, 32, 53	aéroport	空港	Flughafen
airport security staff 16	personnel de sécurité de l'aéroport	空港警備係	Flughafensicherheitspersonal
allergies 56	allergies	アレルギー	Allergien
allowance (duty free) 35	franchise hors taxe	（免税の）許容量	zollfrei
announcement 18	annonce	アナウンス	Bekanntgabe
annual sales conference 45	le briefing annuel	年次販売会議	jährliche Verkaufskonferenz
antiseptic 56	produit antiseptique	消毒薬	Antiseptikum
application form 39	formulaire de demande emploi	応募用紙	Bewerbungsformular
appointment 2, 3	rendezvous	面会の約束	Verabredung
area code 31	code postal	市外局番	Postleitzahl
arrival 4, 18	arrivée	到着	Ankunft
association 67	association	会社	Zusammenarbeit
automatic 52	automatique	オートマチックの	automatisch
baggage 15	bagages	手荷物	Gepäck
baggage claim 33	zone de livraison des bagages	手荷物引き渡し所	Gepäckausgabe
bathroom 9	salle de bains	浴室	Badezimmer
bedroom 9	chambre	寝室	Schlafzimmer
bell captain [UK: head porter] 8, 25	concierge	ボーイ長	Chefpage
bell hop/bell man [UK: porter] 1, 58	porteur	ボーイ、ポーター	Page
bill 1, 24	billet	紙幣	Blatt
binders 27	classeurs	バインダー	Buchbinder
birth date 34	date de naissance	生年月日	Geburtsdatum
board (an airplane) (v) 15	embarquer	搭乗する	einsteigen
boarding pass 15, 32	carte d'embarquement	搭乗券	Bordkarte
boss 20	patron	上司	Chef
breakfast 40	petit déjeuner	朝食	Frühstück
briefcase 16	sacoche	書類かばん	Brieftasche
brochure 28, 46	brochure	パンフレット、小冊子	Prospekt
buffet 40, 70	buffet	ビュッフェ	Buffet
burger 14, 62, 69	burger	ハンバーガー	Burger
business acquaintances 41	connaissances	仕事上の知人	Geschäftsbekanntschaften
business card 41	carte de visite	業務用名刺	Visitenkarte
business contact 41	contact	仕事上の関係者	Geschäftsbeziehung
business lunch 28	déjeuner d'affaires	商談をしながらとる昼食	Geschäftsessen
business services 31, 27, 70	services	ホテルのサービス業務	Geschäftsdienste
business trip 33, 60	voyage d'affaires	出張	Geschäftsreise
cab [UK: taxi] 21, 25, 57	taxi	タクシー	Taxi
cab driver [UK: taxi driver] 1	chauffeur de taxi	タクシーの運転手	Taxifahrer/in

English	Portuguese and Spanish
Common American usage	*Common Latin American usage*
[UK:] = British English	[C:] = Castilian Spanish

PORTUGUESE	ITALIAN	SPANISH	ENGLISH
aceitação	accettazione	aceptación	acceptance 41
acidente	incidente	accidente	accident 54
conta	conto	cuenta	account 27, 70
endereço	indirizzo	dirección	address 33, 34, 38, 47, 56
adulto	adulto	adulto	adult 52
anunciante	inserzionista	anunciante	advertiser 63
publicidade	pubblicità	publicidad	advertising 62, 63
acordo	accordo	acuerdo	agreement 64
ar-condicionado	climatizzato	con aire acondicionado	air conditioned 52
condicionamento de ar	aria condizionata	acondicionamiento de aire	air conditioning 58, 59
correio aéreo	posta aerea	vía aérea	airmail 55
aeroporto	aeroporto	aeropuerto	airport 2, 16, 18, 25, 32, 53
empregados de segurança do aeroporto	personale di sicurezza aeroportuale	oficiales de seguridad del aeropuerto	airport security staff 16
alergias	allergie	alergias	allergies 56
limite de compras isentas de impostos alfandegários	quantità esente da dazio	compras exentas de impuesto aduanero	allowance (duty free) 35
aviso	annuncio	aviso	announcement 18
congresso anual de vendas	conferenza annuale sulle vendite	congreso anual de ventas	annual sales conference 45
antissépticas	antisettico	antiséptico	antiseptic 56
formulário	modulo di domanda d'assunzione	formulario	application form 39
encontro marcado	appuntamento	cita, encuentro	appointment 2, 3
D.D.D.; D.D.N	prefisso	código telefónico regional	area code 31
chegada	arrivo	llegada	arrival 4, 18
associação	associazione	asociación	association 67
(mudança) automática	automatico	(cambio) automático	automatic 52
bagagem	bagaglio	equipaje	baggage 15
retirada de bagagem	zona di ritiro bagaglio	reclamación de equipaje	baggage claim 33
banheiro	stanza da bagno	cuarto de baño	bathroom 9
dormitório	camera da letto	dormitorio	bedroom 9
chefe de portaria 8, 25	capo fattorino	jefe de portería	bell captain [UK: head porter] 8, 25
porteiro	fattorino	botones	bell hop/bell man [UK: porter] 1, 58
nota (de dólar)	banconota	billete	bill 1, 24
pastas classificadoras	rilegatori	carpetas	binders 27
data de nascimento	data di nascita	fecha de nacimiento	birth date 34
embarcar	imbarcarsi	embarcar	board (an airplane) (v) 15
cartão de embarque	carta d'imbarco	tarjeta de embarco	boarding pass 15, 32
chefe	capo	jefe	boss 20
café de manhã	colazione	desayuno	breakfast 40
pasta	borsa ventiquattrore	portafolios	briefcase 16
brochura	opuscolo	folleto	brochure 28, 46
bufé	buffet	bufete	buffet 40, 70
burguer	burger	burguesa	burger 14, 62, 69
pessoas conhecidas por intermédio de negócios	conoscenze di affari	conocidos/conocidas de negocios	business acquaintances 41
cartão comercial	biglietto da visita	tarjeta comercial	business card 41
contato de negócios	contatto di affari	colega comercial	business contact 41
almoço de negócios	pranzo di affari	almuerzo de negocios	business lunch 28
atendimento executivos	servizi d'affari	servicios ejecutivos	business services 31, 27, 70
viagem de negócios	viaggio d'affari	viaje de negocios	business trip 33, 60
taxi	taxi	taxi	cab [UK: taxi] 21, 25, 57
chofer de táxi	tassista	chófer de taxi [c: taxista]	cab driver [UK: taxi driver] 1

ENGLISH	FRENCH	JAPANESE	GERMAN
calendar 3	calendrier	カレンダー	Kalender
call (v) 2	appeler	電話をかける	rufen
camera 16	appareil photo	カメラ	Kamera
candy [UK: sweets] 7	bonbons	キャンディー	Bonbons
capability 46	capacité	能力	Fähigkeit
car 25, 44, 52, 53, 62	voiture	車	Auto
car license-plate 8	plaque d'immatriculation	ナンバープレート	Nummernschild
carafe 12	carafe	デカンター	Karaffe
carry-on luggage 16	bagages à main	機内持込み手荷物	Handgepäck
cash 8, 24, 54, 63	espèces	現金	Bargeld
catalog 6	catalogue	カタログ	Katalog
cellular phone 27	téléphone portable	携帯電話	mobiles Telefon
certificate 39	certificat	免許証、証明書	Zeugnis
change (n) 1, 24	monnaie	つり銭	Wechselgeld
change (v) 24	changer	両替する	wechseln
charge (v) 6, 27	payer par carte	請求する	aufschreiben
charge card 53	carte de crédit	特定の店のクレジットカード	Kreditkarte
check-in 15, 57	enregistrer	搭乗、チェックイン	einchecken
check-out 57, 70	libérer la chambre	チェックアウト	abmelden
Chief Executive 19	P.D.G. (m/f)	最高業務執行者	Geschäftsleiter
children 52	enfants	子供	Kinder
citizenship 34	citoyenneté	市民権	Staatsbürgerschaft
city 24, 53	ville	都市	Stadt
claim (insurance) 33	déclaration de sinistre	保険金請求	Reklamation
coffee 14, 62	café	コーヒー	Kaffee
collate 27	regrouper	ページ順を揃える	vergleichen
colleague 41, 60	collègue	同僚	Kollege/Kollegin
commercial (TV) 63	publicité	コマーシャル	Werbefernsehen
company 5, 19, 28, 33, 43, 44, 68	société	会社	Firma
compatible 55	compatible	適合した	kompatibel
computer 27, 43, 44, 45, 47, 55, 67, 68	ordinateur	コンピューター	Computer
conference 10, 65, 68	conférence	会議	Konferenz
conference center 31	centre de conférences	会議場	Konferenzzentrum
confrontation 57	confrontation	対決	Konfrontation
connecting flight 15,18	vol de correspondance	接続便	Verbindungsflug
connection 18	correspondance	乗り換え	Verbindung
contents 33	contenu	中身	Inhalt
continental breakfast 40	petit déjeuner	コーヒーとパンだけの朝食	kleines Frühstück
contract 4, 10, 19, 28, 55	contrat	契約、契約書	Vertrag
convention 17, 44, 57, 65, 66, 67, 68, 72	conférence	代表者会議	Tagung
conversation 48	conversation	会話	Gespräch
conveyor (belt) 16	tapis roulant	ベルトコンベアー	Fließband
correspondence 39	courier	通信	Korrespondenz
courier 55	courrier	急便	Kurier
courtesy bus 25	navette	送迎バス	gebührenfreier Bus
credit card 8, 24, 32, 54	carte de crédit	クレジットカード	Kreditkarte
customer 57	client	顧客	Kunde/Kundin
customs declaration form 35	formulaire de douane	税関申告書	Zollerklärungsformular
database 46, 47	base de données	データベース	Database

English		**Portuguese and Spanish**	
Common American usage		*Common Latin American usage*	
[UK:] = British English		*[C:] = Castilian Spanish*	

PORTUGUESE	ITALIAN	SPANISH	ENGLISH
calendário	calendario	calendario	calendar 3
chamar	chiamare	llamar	call (v) 2
máquina fotográfica	macchina fotografica	máquina fotográfica	camera 16
balas	caramella	caramelos	candy [UK: sweets] 7
capacidade	capacità	capacidad	capability 46
carro	macchina, automobile	auto [C: coche]	car 25, 44, 52, 53, 62
placa de carro	targa (di automobile)	placa de matrícula	car license-plate 8
jarra	caraffa	jarra	carafe 12
bagagem de mão	bagagli a mano	equipaje de mano	carry-on luggage 16
dinheiro em espécie	contante	dinero en efectivo	cash 8, 24, 54, 63
catálogo	catalogo	catálogo	catalog 6
telefone celular	telefono cellulare	teléfono celular	cellular phone 27
diploma, certificado	certificato	diploma	certificate 39
trocado	cambio	cambio	change (n) 1, 24
trocar	cambiare	cambiar	change (v) 24
cobrar	addebitare	poner en la cuenta	charge (v) 6, 27
cartão de corbrança	carta di credito	tarjeta de crédito	charge card 53
registrar-se	registrarsi	registrarse	check-in 15, 57
pagar a conta e sair	pagare il conto e andarsene	arreglar la cuenta al salir del hotel	checkout (v) 57, 70
Chefe Executive, Presidente	Capo Esecutivo	Ejecutivo Principal	Chief Executive 19
crianças	bambini	niños	children 52
cidadania	cittadinanza	ciudadanía	citizenship 34
cidade	città	ciudad	city 24, 53
pedido reembolso (de seguros)	richiesta di risarcimento	reclamación de seguros	claim (insurance) 33
café	caffè	café	coffee 14, 62
colocar em ordem sequencial	collocare pagine in sequenza	poner las páginas en secuencia	collate 27
colega	collega	colega	colleague 41, 60
comercial (TV)	pubblicità, spot	TV comercial	commercial (TV) 63
empresa	compagnìa, ditta	empresa	company 5, 19, 28, 33, 43, 44, 68
compatível	compatibile	compatible	compatible 55
computador	computer	computador	computer 27, 43, 44, 45, 47, 55, 67, 68
conferência	conferenza	conferencia	conference 10, 65, 68
centro de convenções	centro coferenza	centro de conferencias	conference center 31
confronto	confronto	confrontación	confrontation 57
vôo de conexão	volo di coincidenza	vuelo de enlace	connecting flight 15,18
conexão	coincidenza	enlace	connection 18
conteúdo	contenuto	contenido	contents 33
café de manhã continental	colazione continentale	desayuno tipo continental	continental breakfast 40
contrato	contratto	contrato	contract 4, 10, 19, 28, 55
convenção	congresso	convención	convention 17, 44, 57, 65, 66, 67, 68, 72
conversa	conversazione	conversación	conversation 48
esteira	nastro trasportatore	banda transportadora	conveyor (belt) 16
correspondência	corrispondenza	correspondencia	correspondence 39
serviço de malote	corriere	mensajero	courier 55
ônibus de cortesia	minibus, pulmino	autobús gratuito	courtesy bus 25
cartão de crédito	carta di credito	tarjeta de crédito	credit card 8, 24, 32, 54
cliente	cliente	cliente/a	customer 57
formulário de declaração de alfândega	modulo di dichiarazione della dogana	formulario de declaración aduanera	customs declaration form 35
'database'	'database'	'database' (computadores)	database 46, 47

Wordlist

ENGLISH	FRENCH	JAPANESE	GERMAN
date of birth 38, 56	date de naissance	生年月日	Geburtsdatum
deal 44	affaire	取引	Abkommen
declare (v) 35	déclarer	課税品を申告する	verzollen
degree 39	licence	学位	Diplom
delay (v) 2	retarder	遅らせる	verschieben
deli (delicatessen) 14	.traiteur	デリカテッセン	Delikatessengeschäft
delivery 55	livraison	配達	Lieferung
dentist 56	dentiste	歯科医	Zahnarzt
department 43,45	service	部門	Abteilung
department store 22	grand magasin	デパート	Kaufhaus
departure 4, 18	départ	出発	Abreise
departures board 15	tableau de départ	出発時刻表示板	
deposit 54	acompte	保証金	Anzahlung
description 5	description	種類	Beschreibung
design 68	design	デザイン	Entwurf
desk calendar 4	agenda	卓上カレンダー	Kalender
destination 55	destination	目的地	Reiseziel
dinner 20, 21, 68	dîner	夕食	Abendessen
directions 36	directions	方向	Richtungen
directory assistance 31	renseignements	電話番号案内	Fernsprechauskunft
disk (computer) 46, 55	disk	コンピューターディスク	Diskette
discount 46	remise	割引	Rabatt
display (v) 45	démontrer	展示する	zeigen
distributor 44, 55	distributeur	代理店	Großhändler
disturb (v) 17	déranger	邪魔をする	stören
documents 27, 55	documents	書類	Urkundes
double room 9	chambre à deux personnes	（ホテルの）ダブルの部屋	Doppelzimmer
downtown [UK: city centre] 25, 53	centre ville	中心街	Innenstadt
driver 25, 54	conducteur	運転者	Fahrer
driver's license 24, 38, 53, 54	permis de conduire	運転免許証	Führerschein
driver's test 54	examen du permis de conduire	運転免許試験	Fahrprüfung
drug store [UK: chemist] 22	pharmacie	薬局	Drogerie
duration 15, 70	durée	継続	Länge
education 38, 68	enseignement	教育	Erziehung
electric roof 52	toit ouvrant	（車の）自動サンルーフ	elektrisches Schiebedach
electronic game 17	jeu éléctronique	ビデオゲーム	elektronisches Spiel
elevator [UK: lift] 26	ascenseur	エレベーター	Fahrstuhl
emergency 56	urgence	緊急事態	Notfall
emergency exit 15	sortie de secours	非常口	Notausgang
employer 30	employeur	雇い主	Arbeitgeber
employment 38, 39	emploi	雇用	Angestellte
engineer 58	ingénieur	エンジニア	Ingenieur
evening 21	soir	晩	Abend
excursion 60	sortie	小旅行	Ausflug
executive (business) 48	cadre	重役	Manager/in
exhibition hall 65, 68	salle d'exposition	展示会場	Ausstellungshalle
exhibitor 65, 68	exposant	出品者	Aussteller/in
expenses 70	frais	費用	Kosten
expensive 44, 59	cher	高価な	teuer
experience 59, 60	expérience	経験	Erfahrung
expressway 54	autoroute	高速道路	Schnellstraße

English	Portuguese and Spanish
Common American usage	*Common Latin American usage*
[UK:] = British English	[C:] = Castilian Spanish

PORTUGUESE	ITALIAN	SPANISH	ENGLISH
data de nascimento	data di nascita	fecha de nacimiento	date of birth 38, 56
trato, nagócio	affare	acuerdo de negocios	deal (n) 44
declarar	dichiarare	declarar	declare (v) 35
diploma	diploma di laurea	grado	degree 39
atrasar	ritardare	tardar	delay (v) 2
delicatessen	pasticceria	delicatessen (tienda de fiambres)	deli (delicatessen) 14
entrega	consegna	entrega	delivery 55
dentista	dentista	dentista	dentist 56
departamento	ufficio, reparto	departamento	department 43, 45
loja de departamento	grande magazzino	almacén	department store 22
partida	partenza	salida	departure
painel de partidas	tabellone delle partenze	tabla informativa de salidas	departures board 15
depósito	deposito, conto	depósito	deposit 54
descrição	descrizione	descripción	description 5
desenho	progetto, disegno	proyecto	design
calendário de mesa (de escritório)	agenda da scrivania	almanaque de buró	desk calendar 4
destino	destinazione	destino	destination 55
jantar	cena	cena	dinner 20, 21, 68
informações (para encontrar o caminho certo)	direzioni	direcciones	directions 36
informações sobre assinantes (telefone)	informazione elenco abbonati	servicio de informaciones telefónicas	directory assistance 31
disquete (de computador)	dischetto	disco de computador	disk (computer) 46, 55
desconto	sconto	descuento	discount 46
exibir/expor	esporre	exponer	display (v) 45
distribuidor	distributore	distribuidor/a	distributor 44, 55
incomodar	disturbare	molestar	disturb (v) 17
documentos	documentos	documentos	documents 27, 55
de casal quarto	camera doppia	habitación doble	double room 9
centro	centro	centro	downtown [UK: city centre] 25, 53
motorista	guidatore, autista	conductor	driver 25, 54
carteira de motorista	patente	libreta de manejar	driver's license 24, 38, 53, 54
exame de motorista	esame di guida	test de conducir	driver's test 54
farmácia	farmacia	farmacia	drug store [UK: chemist] 22
duração	durata	duración	duration 15, 70
educação	educazione, istruzione	educación	education 38, 68
capota elétrica	tetto elettrico	techo eléctrico	electric roof 52
jogo electrônico	gioco elettronico	juego eletrónico	electronic game 17
elevador	ascensore	ascensor	elevator [UK: lift] 26
emergência	emergenza	emergencia	emergency 56
saída de emergência	uscita di emergenza	salida de emergencia	emergency exit 15
empregador/a	datore di lavoro	patrón/a	employer 30
emprego	impiego, lavoro	empleo	employment 38, 39
engenheiro	ingegnere	ingeniero	engineer 58
noite	sera	noche	evening 21
excursão	escursione	excursión	excursion 60
executivo/executiva	funzionario d'affari, dirigente	ejecutivo/ejecutiva	executive (business) 48
sala de exposições	sala esposizioni	sala de exposiciones	exhibition hall 65, 68
expositor/a	espositore	expositor/a	exhibitor 65, 68
despesas	spese	gastos	expenses 70
caro	costoso, caro	caro	expensive 44, 59
experiência	esperienza	experiencia	experience 59, 60
auto-estrada	autostrada, superstrada	autopista	expressway 54

ENGLISH	FRENCH	JAPANESE	GERMAN
factory 4, 61	usine	工場	Fabrik
family name [UK: surname] 34	nom de famille 34	姓	Nachname
fax 27, 55	fax	ファックス	Fax
figures 19	chiffres	数字	Zahlen
filling (in tooth) 56	plombage	充填物	Plombe
first name 34	prénom	名	Vorname
flight 15, 18, 33, 35, 50, 57	vol	飛行、飛行機の便	Flug
floppy disk 6, 55	disquette	フロッピーディスク	Diskette
follow 2	suivre	後について行く	folgen
food 29	nourriture	食べ物	Nahrung
form 23, 33	formulaire	用紙	Form
front desk 25, 58, 72	réception	フロント	Rezeption
fuel 52	essence	燃料	Benzin
games 47	jeux	ゲーム	Spiele
gas station [UK: petrol station] 54	station de service	ガソリンスタンド	Tankstelle
graphics 45, 46	graphiques	グラフィック	Zeichnungen
gratuity 1	pourboire	チップ	Trinkgeld
greeting 2, 41	salutation	あいさつ	Gruß
guest 20, 26, 57	invité	宿泊客	Gast
guest registration card 8	fiche d'enregistrement	宿帳	Anmeldeformular
hairdresser 1	coiffeur	美容師	Friseur
hall 26	passage	ホール	Gang
handouts 45	photocopies	配布資料	Photokopien
head office 32	siège	本社	Zentrale
headset 17	casque	ヘッドホン	Kopfhörer
health club 30	gymnase club	ヘルスクラブ	Fitneß-Center
highway 36, 54	autoroute	幹線道路	Landstraße
hotel 24, 25, 26, 27, 44, 57, 59, 61, 65, 70, 72	hotel	ホテル	Hotel
house keeper (maid) 1, 58	femme de chambre	家政婦	Haushälterin
house wine 12	la cuvée du patron	ハウスワイン	Hauswein
ice-cream 13	glace	アイスクリーム	Eiskrem
immigration inspector 34	officiel d'immigration	移民調査官	Beamte/r der Einwanderungsbehörde
imported 12	importé	輸入された	importiert
income 63	salaire	収入	Einkommen
information 45, 47, 60	informations	情報	Information
insurance 33, 53, 54	assurance	保険	Versicherung
international 15	international	国際的	international
interview (v) 39, 4	interviewer	面接する	interviewen
introduce (v) 26, 41	présenter	紹介する	vorstellen
inventory 47	inventaire	目録	Inventar
invitation 41, 61	invitation	招待	Einladung
invoice 6	facture	送り状	Rechnung
itemize (v) 33	spécifier	明細を記す	spezifizieren
itinerary 4, 18	itinéraire	旅程表	Reiseroute
job 5	emploi	仕事	Job
ketchup 13	ketchup	ケチャップ	Ketchup
key 8	clé	鍵	Schlüssel
keyboard 45, 47	clavier	キーボード	Tastatur
lane 54	voie	車線	Spur

English	Portuguese and Spanish
Common American usage	*Common Latin American usage*
[UK:] = British English	[C:] = Castilian Spanish

PORTUGUESE	ITALIAN	SPANISH	ENGLISH
fábrica	fabbrica	fábrica	factory 4, 61
sobrenome	cognome	apellido	family name [UK: surname] 34
fax	fax	fax	fax 27, 55
números	dati, cifre	números	figures 19
obturação	amalgama	obturación	filling 56
nome	nome	nombre de pila	first name 34
vôo	volo	vuelo	flight 15, 18, 33, 35, 50, 57
disquete flexível	dischetto flessibile	disco flexible	floppy disk 6, 55
seguir	seguire	seguir	follow 2
comida	cibo	comida	food 29
formulário	modulo	formulario	form 23, 33
recepção	sportello accettazione clienti	recepción	front desk 25, 58, 72
combustível	benzina	combustible	fuel 52
jogos	giochi	juegos	games 47
posto de gasolina	statzione di benzina	estación de nafta [C: gasolinera]	gas station [UK: petrol station] 54
gráficos	grafici	gráficos	graphics 45, 46
gorjeta	mancia	propina	gratuity 1
saudação	saluto	saludo	greeting 2, 41
hóspede (hotel), convidado/convidada (jantar)	ospite	huésped, invitado/invitada	guest 20, 26, 57
ficha de hóspede	carta di registrazione degli ospiti	ficha de registro de huésped	guest registration card 8
cabeleleiro/a	parrucchiere	peluquero/a	hairdresser 1
corredor	ingresso	corredor	hall 26
folhetos	dichiarazioni per la stampa	folletos	handouts 45
matriz	sede centrale	sede social	head office 32
fone	cuffia	auricular	headset 17
academia de ginástica	palestra	club de gimnasia	health club 30
estrada	autostrada	carretera principal	highway 36, 54
hotel	albergo	hotel	hotel 24, 25, 26, 27, 44, 57, 59, 61, 65, 70, 72
governanta (camareira)	domestica	ama de llaves (camarera)	house keeper (maid) 1, 58
vinho da casa	vino della casa	vino de la casa	house wine 12
sorvete	gelato	helado	ice-cream 13
oficial de imigração	ispettore dell'ufficio immigrazione	oficial de inmigración	immigration inspector 34
importado	importato	importado	imported 12
renda	reddito	salario	income 63
informação	informazioni	información	information 45, 47, 60
seguros	assicurazione	de seguros	insurance 33, 53, 54
internacional	internazionale	internacional	international 15
entrevistar	intervistare	entrevistar	interview (v) 39, 4
apresentar	presentare	presentar	introduce (v) 26, 41
relação	inventario	inventario	inventory 47
convite	invito	invitación	invitation 41, 61
fatura	fattura	factura	invoice 6
relacionar	dettagliare	detallar	itemize (v) 33
itinerãrio	itincrario	itinerario	itinerary 4, 18
emprego	lavoro	empleo	job 5
catchup	salsa ketchup	catchup	ketchup 13
chave	chiave	clave	key 8
teclado	tastiera	teclado	keyboard 45, 47
pista	corsia	pista	lane 54

ENGLISH	FRENCH	JAPANESE	GERMAN
language 38	langue	言語	Sprache
laundry service 70	service pressing	（ホテルの）クリーニング業務	Wäscherei
lawyer 10, 55	avocat	弁護士	Rechtsanwalt
lecture room 65	salle de conférences	講演室	Hörsaal
legibly 35	lisiblement	読みやすいように	lesbar
leisure 47, 64	loisirs	レジャー	Freizeit
limousine 25	limousine	リムジン	Limousine
lobby 25	hall	ロビー	Diele
local specialty 29	spécialité de la région	その土地の名物料理	lokale Spezialität
location 36	endroit	場所	Lage
luggage 16, 25, 52	bagages	手荷物	Gepäck
lunch 4, 18	déjeuner	昼食	Mittagessen
machine 16	machine	機械	Maschine
magazine 7, 63	magazine	雑誌	Zeitschrift
maid 1	bonne	（ホテルの）メイド	Dienstmädchen
main entrance 65	entrée principale	主要玄関	Haupteingang
main hall 65, 68	hall principal	メインホール	Haupthalle
maintenance 58	entretien	管理	Aufrechterhaltung
management 31, 63	direction	経営、経営者	Leitung
manager 2, 57, 63, 72	directeur	マネージャー、部長	Manager/Geschäftsführer
manufacturing plant 24	usine	製造工場	Fabrikationsbetrieb
map 36, 37	carte	地図	Landkarte
market researcher 63	chercheur en marketing	市場調査人	Marktforscher
marketing 5, 45, 63	marketing	マーケティング	Marketing
medical condition 56	condition médicale	健康状態	medizinischer Zustand
medium 63	medium	マスコミ機関	Medium
meeting 4, 27, 61, 63, 72	réunion	会議	Zusammentreffen
menu 29, 40	menu	メニュー	Speisekarte
menu board 13	carte	メニュー表	Speisetafel
micro-cassette 67	mini cassette	マイクロカセットテープレコーダー	Mikrocassette
mineral water 12	eau minérale	ミネラルウォーター	Mineralwasser
mini-bar 59, 70	mini bar	（ホテルの部屋の）ミニバー	Minibar
modem 27, 47, 55	modem	モデム	Modem
money 24, 62, 63	argent	お金	Geld
monochrome 45	monochrome	白黒の	monochrom
mouse (computer) 47	souris	（コンピューターの）マウス	Maus
nationality 5	nationalité	国籍	Staatsangehörigkeit
newspaper 17, 63	journal	新聞	Tageszeitung
newsstand 59	kiosque	新聞雑誌売り場	Zeitungsstand
next of kin 56	personne à prévenir	最近親者	nächste(r) Verwandte(r)
non-smoking 12	non fumeur	禁煙	Nichtraucher
number (phone) 31	numéro	（電話）番号	Telefonnummer
offence (criminal) 54	délit	違反	Straftat
office 19, 26, 37, 41, 43	bureau	オフィス、事務所	Büro
one-way 50	aller simple	一方通行の	Einfach
operator 58	opérateur	交換手	Vermittler/in
order 69	commande	注文	Bestellung
order (v) 6, 69	commander	注文する	bestellen
organizer 68	organisateur	主催者	Organisator/in
overhead projector (O.H.P.) 45	rétroprojecteur	オーバーヘッドプロジェクター	Tageslichtprojektor
overhead transparencies 27	transparents	OHP用フィルム	Transparenten
pack (v) 15	emballer	荷造りする	packen

English	Portuguese and Spanish
Common American usage	Common Latin American usage
[UK:] = British English	[C:] = Castilian Spanish

PORTUGUESE	ITALIAN	SPANISH	ENGLISH
língua	lingua	idioma	language 38
serviço de lavanderia	servizio lavanderia	servicio de lavandería	laundry service 70
advogado/avogada	avvocato	abogado/abogada	lawyer 10, 55
sala de conferências	sala di conferenza	sala de conferencias	lecture room 65
legivelmente	leggibilmente	legiblemente	legibly 35
lazer (adj.), de lazer (n.)	tempo libero	como pasatiempo (adj.), ocio (n)	leisure 47, 64
limusine	limousine	limusina	limousine 25
saguão	hall	zaguán	lobby 25
especialidade regional	specialità della zona	especialidad regional	local specialty 29
lugar	ubicazione	ubicación	location 36
bagagem	bagaglio	equipaje	luggage ¹6, 25, 52
almoço	pranzo	almuerzo	lunch 4, 18
máquina	macchina	aparato	machine 16
revista	rivista	revista	magazine 7, 63
camareira	cameriera	camarera	maid 1
entrada principal	entrata principale	entrada principal	main entrance 65
saguão principal	sala principale	sala principal	main hall 65, 68
manutenção	manutenzione	mantenimiento	maintenance 58
gerência	direzione	dirección	management 31, 63
gerente	dirigente, manager	gerente	manager 2, 57, 63, 72
fábrica	fabbrica	fábrica	manufacturing plant 24
mapa	mappa, cartina	mapa	map 36, 37
pesquisador/a de mercado	ricercatore di mercato	prospector/a de mercado	market researcher 63
marketing	marketing	marketing	marketing 5, 45, 63
doenças anteriores	stato di salute	enfermedades anteriores	medical condition 56
meio de publicidade	media	medio de publicidad	medium 63
reunião	incontro	reunión	meeting 4, 27, 61, 63, 72
cardápio	menu	menú	menu 29, 40
quadro do cardápio	lista del giorno	menú	menu board 13
micro-fita	micro-cassetta	micro cassette	micro-cassette 67
água mineral	acqua minerale	agua mineral	mineral water 12
frigobar	mini-bar	minibar	mini-bar 59, 70
'modem' (de computador)	modem	'módem' (computador)	modem 27, 47, 55
dinheiro	denaro, soldi	dinero	money 24, 62, 63
monocromático	monocromatico	monocromo	monochrome 45
mouse (de computador)	mouse	ratón (computador)	mouse (computer) 47
nacionalidade	nazionalità	nacionalidad	nationality 5
jornal	quotidiano, giornale	diario	newspaper 17, 63
banca de jornais	edicola	quiosco de periódicos	newsstand 59
parente mais próximo	parente più stretto	pariente más cercano/a	next of kin 56
não-fumante	non fumatori	no-fumador	non-smoking 12
número	numero (telefono)	número	number (phone) 31
delito	reato	delito	offence (criminal) 54
escritório	ufficio	oficina	office 19, 26, 37, 41, 43
(passagem) de ida	solo andata	de ida	one-way 50
telefonista	operatore	telefonista	operator 58
pedido	ordine	pedido	order 69
pedir	ordinare	pedir	order (v) 6, 69
organizador/a	organizzatore	organizador/a	organizer 68
retroprojetor	lavagna luminosa	retroproyector	overhead projector (O.H.P.) 45
transparências de retroprojetor	lucidi per lavagna luminosa	transparencias para retroproyector	overhead transparencies 27
fazer as malas	fare le valigie	hacer la maleta	pack (v) 15

ENGLISH	FRENCH	JAPANESE	GERMAN
package (parcel) 23	paquet	小包	Paket
package (software) 46	package	既製プログラム	Softwarepaket
participant 65, 68	participant	参加者	Teilnehmer/in
passengers 15, 18	passagers	乗客	Fahrgäste
passport 24, 34	passeport	パスポート	Reisepaß
personal data/information 35, 39	renseignements personals	個人情報	persönliche Informationen
phone 30, 55, 59	téléphone	電話	Telefon
photocopy (v) 27	photocopier	コピーをとる	photokopieren
place of birth 38	lieu de naissance	出生地	Geburtsort
plane 2, 17, 18, 72	avion	飛行機	Flugzeug
planner 68	planner	立案者	Agenda
pocket 16	poche	ポケット	Tasche
polite 57	poli	丁重な	höflich
political 17	politique	政党の	politisch
politician 17	homme politique	政治家	Politiker/in
population 45, 63	population	人口	Bevölkerung
portable phone 17	téléphone portable	携帯電話	tragbares Telefon
post office 23	bureau de poste	郵便局	Postamt
postage 55	affranchissement	郵便料	Postgebühr
presentation 45, 68	présentation	説明、紹介	Uberreichung/Darbietung
price 46	prix	価格	Preis
printer 47	imprimante	プリンター	Drucker
product 7	produit	製品	Produkt
production 5	production	製造	Herstellung
productivity 64	productivité	生産性	Produktivität
profession 66	profession	職業	Beruf
professional 63	professionel	専門家	beruflich
program (computer) 45, 46	program	プログラム	Programm
programmer 67	programmeur	コンピュータープログラマー	Programmierer/in
prohibited 15	interdit	禁止されている	verboten
qualification 39	diplôme	資格	Qualifikation
radio 52	radio	ラジオ	Radio
reception 65, 68	réception	受付	Empfang
receptionist 59	réceptioniste	受付係	Empfangsdame
recipient 55	destinataire	受信者	Empfänger
refuse (v) 61	refuser	断わる	ablehnen
regular 7	régulier	通常の	regelmäßig
rent (v) 54	louer	借りる	mieten
rental [UK: hire] 27, 52, 53	location	賃貸の	Mietbetrag
report 19	rapport	報告書	Bericht
representative 2, 19, 38	représentant	代表者	Vertreter
reservation 12, 31	réservation	予約	Reservierung
responsibility 64	responsabilité	責任	Verantwortung
rest room [UK: public toilet] 65	toilettes	(公共の建物の) トイレ	öffentliche Toilette
restaurant 8, 12, 22, 30, 36, 59, 65, 68	restaurant	レストラン	Restaurant
restriction 50	restriction	制限	Beschränkung
resume [UK: curriculum vitae] 38	résumé	履歴書	Resumee
robe 58 [UK: dressing gown]	peignoir	バスローブ	Bademantel
room 8, 57, 58, 67, 69	chambre	部屋	Zimmer

English *Common American usage* [UK:] = British English	Portuguese and Spanish *Common Latin American usage* [C:] = Castilian Spanish

PORTUGUESE	ITALIAN	SPANISH	ENGLISH
pacote	pacchetto	paquete	package (parcel) 23
pacote (de software de computador)	confezione (software)	paquete (de programas–ordenadores)	package (software) 46
participante	partecipante	participante	participant 65, 68
passageiros	passeggeri	pasajeros	passengers 15, 18
passaporte	passaporto	pasaporte	passport 24, 34
informações pessoais	particolari	información personal	personal data/information 35, 39
telefone	telefono	teléfono	phone 30, 55, 59
fotocopiar	fotocopiare	fotocopiar	photocopy (v) 27
lugar de nascimento	luogo di nascita	lugar de nacimiento	place of birth 38
avião	aereo	avión	plane 2, 17, 18, 72
cronograma (de congresso)	programma	horario	planner 68
bolso	tasca	bolsillo	pocket 16
polidas	cortese	cortés	polite 57
político	politico	político	political 17
político (a pessoa)	uomo politico, statista	político/política	politician 17
população	popolazione	población	population 45, 63
telefone portátil	telefono portatile	teléfono portátil	portable phone 17
agência de correio	ufficio postale	correo	post office 23
porte postal	affrancatura	porte de correos	postage 55
apresentação	presentazione	presentación	presentation 45, 68
preço	prezzo	precio	price 46
impressora	stampante	impresora	printer 47
produto	prodotto	producto	product 7
produção	produzione	producción	production 5
produtividade	produttività	productividad	productivity 64
profissão	professione	profesión	profession 66
profissional	professionale	profesional	professional 63
programa	programma	programa	program (computer) 45, 46
programador/a	programmatore	programador/a	programmer 67
proibido	proibito	prohibido	prohibited 15
qualificação	qualificazione	calificación [C: requisito]	qualification 39
rádio	radio	radio	radio 52
recepção	ricezione	recepción	reception 65, 68
recepcionista	addetto alla ricezione	recepcionista	receptionist 59
destinatário	recipiente	destinatorio	recipient 55
recusar	rifiutare	rechazar	refuse (v) 61
normal	regolare	normal	regular 7
alugar	noleggiare	alquilar	rent (v) 54
aluguel	noleggio	alquiler	rental [UK: hire] 27, 52, 53
relatório	rapporto	informe	report 19
representante	rappresentante	representante	representative 2, 19, 38
reserva	prenotazione	reservación	reservation 12, 31
responsibilidade	responsabilità	responsibilidad	responsibility 64
banheiro publica	bagni pubblici	lavabo	rest room [UK: public toilet] 65
restaurante	ristorante	restaurante	restaurant 8, 12, 22, 30, 36, 59, 65, 68
restrição	restrizione	restricción	restriction 50
curriculum vitae	curriculum	resumen	resume [UK: curriculum vitae] 38
roupão	accappatoio	albornoz	robe 58 [UK: dressing gown]
quarto de hotel	stanza, camera	habitación de hotel	room 8, 57, 58, 67, 69

ENGLISH	FRENCH	JAPANESE	GERMAN
room charge 70	prix de la chambre	（ホテルの）部屋代	Zimmergebühr
room service 40, 58, 69	service (de chambre)	ルームサービス	Zimmerservice
round-trip ticket 50	billet aller et retour	往復切符	Rundfahrtkarte
rules 20	règles	規則	Regeln
sales 45	ventes	売上	Verkauf
sales manager 2	directeur de ventes	販売部長	Verkaufsleiter
sales representative 19, 38	représentant	セールスマン	Verkaufsvertreter/in
sales tax 40	taxe de vente	売上税	Verkaufssteuer
sandwich 14	sandwich	サンドイッチ	Sandwich
satellite TV 9	télévision par satellite	衛星放送	Satallitefernsehen
sauna 26	sauna	サウナ	Sauna
scanner (airport) 16	scanner	スキャナー（空港）	Abtaststrahl
scanner (computer) 46, 47	scanner	スキャナー（コンピューター）	Scanner
screen 45	écran	（コンピューターの）画面	Bildschirm
seat assignment 15	attribution de siège	座席割当て	Sitzanweisung
seat belt 18	ceinture de sécurité	シートベルト	Sicherheitsgürtel
seating preference 15	préférence	座席の好み	Sitzvorliebe
secretary 4, 65, 66, 67, 72	secrétaire	秘書	Sekretärin
security check 16	contrôle de sécurité	ボディーチェック	Sicherheitskontrolle
service 57	service	業務	Dienst
service charge 40	service	サービス料	Bearbeitungsgebühr
shopping 22	shopping	買い物	Einkäufe
shower 58	douche	シャワー	Dusche
shuttle bus 25	navette	近距離往復バス	Pendelbus
side order 40	plat d'accompagnement	添え料理の注文	Beilage
signature 40	signature	署名	Unterschrift
single room 9	chambre simple	1人部屋	Einzelzimmer
smoke (v) 12, 15, 18	fumer	たばこを吸う	rauchen
smugglers 35	contrebandiers	密輸人	Schmuggler
soda [UK: soft drinks] 7, 62	boisson gazeuse	炭酸清涼飲料	Brause
software 38, 44, 45, 47	software	ソフトウェア	Software
souvenir 70	souvenir	記念品	Andenken
speaker 65, 68	speaker	発表者	Sprecher/in
special 13	plat du jour	特別料理	Tagesangebot
special offer 32	offre spécial	特別提供	Sonderangebot
specialist 67	spécialiste	専門家	Spezialist
specialty 22, 29	spécialité	自慢料理	Spezialität
speech 66, 67	discours	スピーチ	Rede
speed limit 54	limitation de vitesse	制限速度	Geschwindigkeitsbegrenzung
spreadsheet 46, 47	tableau	スプレッドシート	Buchführungstabelle
stapled 27	agrafé	ホッチキスでとめた	zusammengeheftet
store 22, 24, 47	magasin	店	Kaufhaus
suitcase 33, 35	valise	スーツケース	Koffer
supplement 52	supplément	追加	Ergänzung
supply (v) 47	fournir	供給する	liefern
survey 47	sondage	調査	Umfrage
system 44	système	システム	System
take off 18	décoller	離陸する	starten, abfliegen
tank (fuel) 52	éservoir	ガソリンタンク	Tank
tax 52, 70	impôt	税金	Steuer
taxi (cab) 1, 25	taxi	タクシー	Taxi
telephone 9, 56, 70	téléphone	電話	Telefon

English		**Portuguese and Spanish**	
Common American usage		*Common Latin American usage*	
[UK:] = British English		[C:] = Castilian Spanish	

PORTUGUESE	ITALIAN	SPANISH	ENGLISH
diária	prezzo della camera	precio de habitación	room charge 70
serviço de copa	servizio in camera	servicio de habitación	room service 40, 58, 69
passagem de ida e volta	biglietto andata e ritorno	boleto de viaje redondo [C: billete de ida y vuelta]	round-trip ticket 50
normas	regole	normas	rules 20
vendas	vendite	ventas	sales 45
gerente de vendas	direttore commerciale	jefe de ventas	sales manager 2
representante de vendas	rappresentante	representante de ventas	sales representative 19, 38
imposto sobre vendas	tassa di vendita	impuesto sobre las ventas	sales tax 40
sanduíche	panino	bocadillo	sandwich 14
TV por satélite	TV satellite	TV por satélite	satellite TV 9
sauna	sauna	sauna	sauna 26
dispositivo de detecção	relevatore de i metalli	aparato de detección	scanner (airport) 16
escaneador	scanner	escáner (computador)	scanner (computer) 46, 47
tela	schermo	pantalla	screen 45
reserva de assento	numerazione posto	reservación de asiento	seat assignment 15
cinto de segurança	cintura di sicurezza	cinturón de seguridad	seat belt 18
preferência por assento	dove preferisce sedersi	preferéncia por asiento	seating preference 15
secretária	segretaria	secretaria	secretary 4, 65, 66, 67, 72
controle de segurança	controllo di sicurezza	revista de seguridad	security check 16
serviço	servizio	servicio	service 57
taxa de serviço	servizio	tasa de servicio	service charge 40
compras	shopping	compras	shopping 22
chuveiro	doccia	ducha	shower 58
ônibus de cortesia	pulmino	autobús de cortesia	shuttle bus 25
porção	contorno	ración extra	side order 40
assinatura	firma	firma	signature 40
quarto de sotteiro	camera singola	cuarto sencillo [C: habitación individual]	single room 9
fumar	fumare	fumar	smoke (v) 12, 15, 18
contrabandistas	contrabbandieri	contrabandistas	smugglers 35
refrigerante	aqua brillante	gaseosa	soda [UK: soft drinks] 7, 62
software (computadores)	software	'software' (computador)	software 38, 44, 45, 47
lembrança	ricordo	recuerdo	souvenir 70
palestrante	conferenziere	conferenciante	speaker 65, 68
especial	speciale	especial	special 13
promoção	offerta speciale	oferta especial	special offer 32
especialista	specialista	especialista	specialist 67
especialidade	specialità	especialidad	specialty 22, 29
discurso	discorso	discurso	speech 66, 67
limite de velocidade	limite di velocità	límite de velocidad	speed limit 54
'spreadsheet' (computadores)	spreadsheet	hoja de cálculo	spreadsheet 46, 47
grampeado	cucito	sujetado con grapas	stapled 27
loja	negozio	tienda, almacén	store 22, 24, 47
mala	valigia	maleta	suitcase 33, 35
suplemento	supplemento	suplemento	supplement 52
fornecer	fornire	suministrar	supply (v) 47
pesquisa	sondaggio	cuestionario	survey 47
sistema	sistema	sistema	system 44
decolar	decollare	despegar	take off (v) 18
tanque de combustível	serbatoio (benzina)	tanque (de combustible)	tank (fuel) 52
imposto	tassa	tasa	tax 52, 70
taxi	taxi	taxi	taxi (cab) 1, 25
telefone	telefono	teléfono	telephone 9, 56, 70

ENGLISH	FRENCH	JAPANESE	GERMAN
telephone number 38, 39	numero de téléphone	電話番号	Telefonnummer
television campaign 62	campagne	テレビキャンペーン	Fernsehaktion
temperature 23	température	気温	Temperatur
theater 51	théâtre	劇場	Theater
ticket 15, 25	billet	切符	Fahrkarte
time zone 37	zone horaire	（同一標準時を用いる）時間帯	Zeitzone
tip 1	pourboire	チップ	Trinkgeld
toll free 60	gratuit	無料通話	kostenlos
topic 48	sujet	話題	Thema
traffic 2, 54	circulation	交通	Verkehr
train 36	train	列車	Zug
training 68	formation	訓練	Ausbildung
transfer desk 15, 18	comptoir de transit	乗換え手続カウンター	Transferschalter
travel (v) 18, 20, 44	voyager	旅行する	reisen
travelers check 24, 54	cheque de voyage	旅行者用小切手	Reisescheck
trip 2, 69	voyage	旅行	Fahrt
trunk (of car) [UK: boot] 52	coffre	トランクルーム	Kofferraum
turn off (v) 17	éteindre	消す	abschalten
TV remote control 70	télécommande	テレビのリモコン	Fernsehfernsteuerung
unemployed 64	chômeurs	失業者	Arbeitslosen
vacancies 8	chambres libres	空き部屋	freie Zimmer
vacation 1, 26, 38, 48, 49	vacances	休暇	Ferien
vegetarian 51, 69	végétarien	菜食主義者（の）	Vegetarier/in
vehicle 52	véhicule	乗物	Fahrzeug
video 45	magnétoscope	ビデオ	Video
visit 70	visite	滞在	Besuch
visitor 61	visiteur	訪問者	Besucher/in
waiter 1, 12, 58	serveur	ウェイター	Kellner
washroom 9 [UK: toilet]	toilettes	（公共の建物の）トイレ	Toilette
water 58	eau	水	Wasser
wealthy 63	riche	裕福な	reich
weather 10, 28	temps	天気	Wetter
week 17	semaine	週	Woche
wine list 12	carte des vins	ワインリスト	Weinliste
word processor 46, 62	traitement de texte	ワープロ	Textverarbeitungsanlage
working conditions 64	conditions de travail	労働条件	Arbeitsbedingungen
workshop 68	atelier	研修会	Seminar
zip code [UK: postcode] 33	code postal	郵便番号	Postleitzahl

English		Portuguese and Spanish	
English		**Portuguese and Spanish**	
Common American usage		*Common Latin American usage*	
[UK:] = British English		*[C:] = Castilian Spanish*	

PORTUGUESE	ITALIAN	SPANISH	ENGLISH
número de telefone	numero di telefono	número de teléfono	telephone number 38, 39
campanha de TV	campagna televisiva	campaña de TV	television campaign 62
temperatura	temperatura	temperatura	temperature 23
teatro	teatro	teatro	theater 51
passagem	biglietto	boleto [C: billete]	ticket 15, 25
fuso horário	fuso orario	huso horario	time zone 37
gorjeta	mancia	propina	tip 1
isento de padágio	gratuito	gratuito	toll free 60
tópico	argomento	tema	topic 48
trânsito	traffico	tránsito	traffic 2, 54
trem	treno	tren	train 36
treinamento	formazione	formación	training 68
balcão de conexões	sportello passageri in transito	mostrador de transbordo	transfer desk 15, 18
viajar	viaggiare	viajar	travel (v) 18, 20, 44
cheques de viagem	travelers check	cheque de viaje	travelers check 24, 54
viagem	viaggio	viaje	trip 2, 69
porta-malas	bagagliai	portaequipaje	trunk (of car) [UK: boot] 52
desligar	spengere	apagar	turn off (v) 17
controle remoto da TV	telecomando	mando a distancia	TV remote control 70
desempregado	disoccupato	desempleado	unemployed 64
vagas	camere libere	vacantes	vacancies 8
férias	vacanze	vacaciones	vacation 1, 26, 38, 48, 49
vegetariano/vegetariana	vegetariano	vegetariano/vegetariana	vegetarian 51, 69
veículo	veicolo	vehículo	vehicle 52
vídeo	video	video	video 45
visita	visita	visita	visit 70
hospede	visitatore	visitante	visitor 61
garçom	cameriere	mozo	waiter 1, 12, 58
banheiro	bagno	lavabo	washroom 9 [UK: toilet]
água	acqua	agua	water 58
rico	ricco	adinerado	wealthy 63
tempo	tempo	tiempo	weather 10, 28
semana	settimana	semana	week 17
lista de vinhos	lista dei vini	lista de vinos	wine list 12
processador de texto	trattamento testi	procesador de texto	word processor 46, 62
condições de trabalho	condizioni di lavoro	condiciones de trabajo	working conditions 64
'workshop', seminário	seminario	taller de trabajo	workshop (seminar) 68
C.E.P.	codice postale	código de dirección postal	zip code [UK: postcode] 33

Heinemann English Language Teaching
A division of Heinemann Publishers (Oxford) Ltd.
Halley Court, Jordan Hill, Oxford OX2 8EJ

OXFORD MADRID ATHENS PARIS FLORENCE
PRAGUE SÃO PAULO CHICAGO MELBOURNE
AUCKLAND SINGAPORE TOKYO GABORONE
IBADAN JOHANNESBURG PORTSMOUTH (NH)

ISBN 0 435 29642 6

Additional material written by Anne Delestrée
Designed by Shireen Nathoo Design
Commissioned photography by Sue Baker
Illustrations by: Richard Draper, Susannah English, John Gilkes, Andy Nightingale.

Cover design by Shireen Nathoo Design
Cover photography by: Tony Stone Worldwide/David Joel; Sue Baker

The authors would like to thank their editors at Heinemann both for their enthusiasm and for their very significant contributions to Survival English. In particular we would like to thank Michael Boyd, Valerie Gossage and Louise Spencely for their creative input. We would also like to thank Karen Viney for her comments.

The publishers would like to thank Akemi Katayama, Bärbel Vosgröne, Dawn Ellis, and Peter McCabe for their work on the Wordlist, and Mandy Twells, Maureen Cowdroy, the Richmond Hill Hotel, the Moat House Hotel, Michelin House, U.S.A.F. Upper Heyford, and Lower Croughton High School, for their help with location and other photography.

We would also like to thank the following for their permission to reproduce photographs:
Access Brand Ltd, (8); Ace Photo Agency, (14); Adams Picture Library, (58); American Express Europe Limited, (8); Apple Computer Ltd., (46); Art Directors Photo Library, (7, 58); Aspect Picture Library, (49, 54); Camera Press, (5); Colorsport, (61); Comstock, (18, 38, 64, 67); The Diners Club Limited, (8); Ferrero Rocher, (32); General Motors Corporation, (52); Glenfiddich Distillery, (32); Sally & Richard Greenhill, (Intro); Robert Harding Picture Library, (38, 49); The Hutchinson Library, (22); The Image Bank, (1, 15, 25, 48, 58, 66); Impact Photos, (1, 29); Mastercard International Inc., (8); Perrier (UK) Ltd., (12); Rex Features, (5); Science Photo Library, (16); Spreckley Pittham Limited, (44); Syndication International, (5); Telegraph Colour Library, (Intro, 33); Tony Stone Images, (11, 46, 49, 50, 58, 63); VISA, the Three Brands Design, the Dove Design, PLUS and the Plus Design are registered trade marks of Visa International and are reproduced with permission, (8); Zefa, (16, 29, 60).

Printed and bound in Spain by Cayfosa

94 95 96 97 98 10 9 8 7 6 5 4 3 2 1

Survival English consists of:	
Student's Book	ISBN 0 435 29642 6
Practice Book	ISBN 0 435 29644 2
Teacher's File	ISBN 0 435 29645 0
Cassettes (pack of 2)	ISBN 0 435 29643 4
Double CD Pack	ISBN 0 435 29647 7